Simply Sous Vide

Cindy Kowalyk

Simply Sous Vide

Printed in the United States of America.
First printing: 2011

Disclaimer

This publication contains the opinions and ideas of its author. It is sold with the understanding that the author and publisher are not engaged in tendering cooking or health services in this book. The reader should consult his or her own medical and health providers as appropriate before adopting the cooking method in this book or drawing inferences from it. It is not recommended for those individuals who may have immune problems.

The author and publisher specifically disclaim all responsibility for any liability, loss or risk, personal or otherwise, which is incurred as a consequence, directly or indirectly, of the use and application of any of the contents of this book.

The author and publisher have not received remuneration for mentioning of companies and or products.

Acknowledgements

I would like to thank my husband Ken, and my parents Ed and Madeline Barrett, for their support, encouragement and great taste buds.

Special thanks to my friend, Chef Mark Alba, who introduced me to the sous vide method of cooking. If I had not had the wonderful opportunity of enjoying one of his delicious dishes, I would have missed out on a whole lot of fun and a very rewarding experience.

Preface

Once upon a time there was a fabulous restaurant with an equally fabulous Executive Chef. The Chef was ahead of his time in many ways. He was able to produce the most succulent and delicious rack of lamb. This lamb was like none other and many a diner pondered as to how he was able to produce perfectly cooked lamb each and every time.

But wait this is not a fairy tale! It really happened. The restaurant is in Atlanta, Georgia. The talented Chef exists! Chef introduced me to the Sous Vide method. He showed me this mysterious machine and explained to me how it was possible to prepare and hold his delectable lamb. The machine was quite pricey for a home cook like myself. I was very disappointed that I would not have the pleasure of cooking using this new amazing method. Much to my surprise, I was able to find a company that sold reasonably priced equipment. My equipment arrived and I began to look for recipes. Sadly, all I found were very complex recipes more adapted for a professional chef rather than someone like myself. So began my journey to create recipes which everyone would be able to produce easily with everyday ingredients.

Entertaining family and friends has always been a great passion of mine, however I did not enjoy being in the kitchen while the party was happening without me. Occasionally, a dear friend or family member would arrive late to the party and I would watch my food which was moist and delectable turn into a dried out shoe. Oh well. Cleaning all those pots and pans was never anything I looked forward to with anticipation either!

Sous Vide cooking is fun. Using this method in my day to day cooking has eliminated all of the little worries and tribulations. It has made my life easy. Enjoying the party with my guests is something I am able to do every time. It is my wish for you that your lives be enriched by this wonderful method as well. Enjoy!

Please visit the website www.simplysousvidecooking.com for color photographs as well as more how to's and fun extras which will aide you in using the simply sous vide technique everyday.

Table of Contents

Disclaimer   3
Acknowledgements   4
Preface   5
Table of Contents   7
Introduction   8
Equipment   10
Simply Sous Vide Technique   11
Tips & Facts   14
Soup & Starter Recipes   17
Brunch Recipes   40
Sandwich & Burger Recipes   59
Meat Recipes & Cooking Tables   75
PoultryRecipes & Cooking Tables   116
Seafood Recipes & Cooking Tables   141
Side Dish Recipes   166
Sauce Recipes   203
Pastry Recipes   210
Dessert Recipes   216
Index   240

Introduction

What is sous vide? The sous vide way of cooking was invented in the 1970's. Basically, food is placed in a food grade safe bag. The air is removed from the bag with a vacuum machine. The bag is sealed. The food in the bag is submerged in a temperature controlled water bath where it will cook to perfection.

The patent pending Simply Sous Vide Technique brings sous vide cooking to another level. This novel technique uses containers. Previously, it was not thought possible to create dishes which required form such as cakes, casseroles, etc.

What are the health benefits? The food that is cooked in the sous vide method is never heated above boiling, therefore the nutritious portion of the food is not destroyed due to high heat. The flavor is also locked inside and will not dissipate. All of the vitamins and minerals are retained within the bag.

What are the advantages to use the sous vide method of cooking? Besides the health benefits, sous vide also enables you to hold dinner. In other words, it is not possible to over cook the food. The temperature of the water bath is set to the desired doneness of the food. This is accomplished by setting the water bath to the determined internal temperature of the food being cooked. For example, if a medium rare steak is desired, the internal temperature is between 128° to 131°. The water bath is set to that temperature and because the temperature will never be exceeded, the food will never over cook. This enables you to hold food until you are ready to serve.

Flavor is not lost. Unlike other methods of cooking, the flavor of the food is maintained within the bag. The vacuum process causes the food to intensify in flavor because the juices are not lost. The juices actually baste the food. The food is being cooked at a low heat over a period of time which allows the flavors to develop.

More bang for your buck. The low heat process of the sous vide method will not cause food to shrink. Medium rare steaks and hamburgers are almost the same size after cooking as they were before cooking. Meat that is generally tough can be made to taste like the most tender cut of expensive meats by cooking at a low temperature. Buying inexpensive cuts such as flank steak and cooking it in the sous vide method will duplicate the taste of a wonderful prime rib at a fraction of the cost.

The sous vide method does not require high heat like an ordinary oven and only uses minimum energy. It literally costs pennies to run and will not heat up the house.

It is possible to cook a week or more worth of meals. With a little planning, entire meals can be cooked and then refrigerated or frozen. The convenience of simply re-heating entire meals from appetizers to desserts is amazing. Dinner parties are now easy. Instead of toiling away in the kitchen you are able to enjoy the party and your guests.

The clean up is now made easy. There are no extra dishes to wash or pots to scrub. Just remove the food from the bag and serve. Using the Simply Sous Vide Technique allows you to serve your dinner directly from the water oven to the table. Clean up is a breeze.

For those who reside in small spaces, the equipment takes up little room. Perfect for college students who love to cook! For those who live in condos, your neighbors will never smell what you are cooking for dinner.

Equipment

The necessary equipment to successfully use the sous vide method requires a vacuum machine (which has a manual pulse ability), food grade safe plastic bags (made specifically for this process), a water bath (which can be accurately temperature controlled), and an instant read food thermometer which will double check the temperature of the water bath and the internal temperature of the cooked food. That is all.

Recently, a few sous vide machines have entered the marketplace for the home cook. Sous Vide Magic uses a rice cooker with a controller. Sous Vide Supreme is contained within one unit. Polyscience uses an immersion circulator in conjunction with a water bath (any container which may contain water).

The Sous Vide Magic can be used with a large commercial rice cooker which will enable larger amounts of food to be cooked. The Sous Vide Supreme has a racking system that will allow food to be stacked. Polyscience may be used with any size container which will retain heat.

Simply Sous Vide Technique

The patent pending Simply Sous Vide Technique incorporates every day dishware/containers with food grade safe bags. These dishes can be made of metal, glass, stoneware, plastic, etc. Basically, any dishware which has the ability to conduct heat may be used. The only stipulation is that the container must fit within the food grade safe bag.

There are great benefits to using the Simply Sous Vide Technique. It is possible to serve directly to the table since your serving dishware/container contains your food. You may now create meals which are layered. Previously, it was not thought possible to create dishes which required form such as cakes, casseroles, etc. Soups may be cooked.

It is necessary to have a vacuum machine that removes the air by manually pulsing. This machine enables you to have a seal that will close in around your dish tightly but will have the ability to stop before the contents are sucked into the machine or are crushed.

To use the Simply Sous Vide Technique, select a dish which will fit within the food grade safe bag. Prepare the bag by double sealing one end of the bag (see tips). Prepare the recipe. Place the container inside the bag. Place the open end of the bag in the machine which removes the air. Manually pulse the vacuum machine until a tight seal forms around the container. Seal. Move the bag up slightly from the seal and seal again. The bag has now been sealed four times.

To prevent the liquid part of the recipe from overflowing, try to place a solid element of the recipe on top. This acts as a barrier. It is not always necessary to have a barrier. Such is the case when preparing a soup. Should some liquid overflow from the container into the bag, simply remove the container (after it has finished cooking) from the bag and pour the excess liquid back into the container. Wipe off the dish and serve.

When preparing eggs or other delicate foods, allow gentle pressure from the bag to press down on the food. If over pulsing occurs the egg yolk will break.

The Simply Sous Vide technique will allow you to make your favorite dishes. Your favorites will be enhanced not only in flavor but will be healthier. No more fear of over cooking. Enjoy!

Step By Step Pictures

STEP 1: Seal the end of the bag twice

STEP 2 Make sure there is adequate length for the container to be sealed in

STEP 3: Place open end of the bag into the vacumn machine

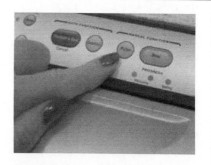

STEP 4: Use the pulse button to remove the air from the bag

STEP 5: Allow the bag to tighten around the container and press down on the food within

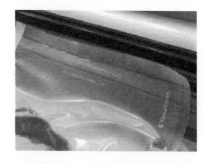

STEP 6: Seal the bag twice. The bag has been sealed a total of four times. Place the bag in the water bath and weight down with a plate.

Tips & Facts

1) Only use bags that are food grade safe and made for cooking using the sous vide method.

2) Always double seal the bags on both ends to ensure the food is properly sealed. This is done by sealing the bottom of the bag once and again a little further from the original seal. Place the food in the bag, remove the air and seal. Seal the bag again a little further from that seal. The bag has been sealed four times. This ensures the food will not be contaminated by the water bath should a seal not hold.

SETTING THE WATER TEMPERATURE

1) Always check the temperature of the water. An instant read thermometer, such as a Thermapen, will ensure the water bath temperature is accurate.

2) Always check the cooking times and temperatures for food by referring to the cooking tables.

COOKING

1) The cooking times on the cooking tables are for the minimal amount of time necessary to cook the food. The food can be held longer if so desired. Note that some food will have a distinct texture change if cooked longer. For example, chicken cooked longer than two hours beyond the minimal time, will tend to become softer. Extending the time beyond two hours may result in a very soft texture. Fish should not be held longer then 30 minutes beyond the minimal time as it too will become overly soft. Flank steak may be cooked for up to 12 to 14 hours. The texture becomes too soft after that amount of time.

2) Always put the food into the bag when it is cold. This prevents bacteria from forming inside the bag and also ensures that the food will be cooked at the proper temperature.

3) Always make sure the bags are submerged in the water. If necessary, weight down with plates.

4) Searing meats such as steaks, rack of lamb, etc. is best done before cooking in the water bath. The reason is two part. First, it imparts a grilled flavor to the meat as well as eliminates a greenish color which may occur on the meat. Second, part of the beauty of using the sous vide method is the ability to be a guest at your own party. If you have a large quantity of meat to sear it must be done in batches and held in a regular oven. By placing the food in a regular oven you risk over cooking your perfectly cooked food! Searing afterwards takes time away from being with your guests.

5) Sear the skin of poultry at the end of cooking. This will ensure a crispy skin. This is best done under a preheated broiler when multiple breasts need to be browned.

6) A kitchen torch is recommended for searing most foods. The kitchen torch will only sear the surface of the food whereas a broiler may over cook the food. A hot skillet is preferable for searing meat if there are large quantities.

7) For re-heating multiple food items (which were cooked at different temperatures), always set the water bath for the lowest setting. This will keep foods from over cooking.

8) Rapid chill. If the food is not to be served immediately, it must be rapidly chilled. This is done by placing cooked food (still in the bag) into an ice bath. The bath should be mostly ice with some water. It must be totally submerged. Keep the food in the ice bath for one hour. Remove from bath and refrigerate or freeze the food which is still in the bag. This must also be done for cakes and cheesecakes in order to set, however, only for thirty minutes if it will be served immediately. Use a cooler or fill up a deep sink if large quantities of food need to be rapid chilled.

9) When food such as flank steak produces liquid/juices after cooking, snip off the corner of the bag and drain the liquid. Reserve for au jus or gravy or discard. You may also reseal the corner (do not try to remove the air) and place the bag back into the water bath to keep warm while you are preparing the au jus or gravy.

10) Do not add sauce to delicate fish as it will make the fish disintegrate. Cook your sauces separately in another bag. Rapid chill any extra fish that has been cooked and which you will reheat for another meal. Rapid chill the cooked sauce as well. Place both sealed bags (fish and sauce) into one bag. Mark on the outside of the bag the contents, date, and the lowest temperature. Upon reheating, both your fish and sauce will be heated at the same time.

11) Heat your serving plates (know what temperature the plates are allowed to be heated to) in a low oven 175° to 200°. This will enable the sous vide food to remain warm after plating.

FOOD

1) Some foods will not taste appetizing when using the sous vide method. For example, a strong tasting fish will become more concentrated in flavor. Eggplant and Rutabaga contain bitter juices. In a conventional oven, these juices will dissipate and carmelize with the heat. The sous vide method will concentrate the bitterness. Cook these vegetables in a regular oven first, and incorporate them into sous vide dish.

2) Fresh fish should be placed in the freezer for 20 minutes to 30 minutes. This will kill any parasites which may be in the fish.

3) Cook sauces which contain wine before incorporating into a recipe. By not doing so may impart a strong alcohol flavor, thus overwhelming the dish. Always cool your warm sauces before adding to foods which will be cooked in the sous vide method.

4) Always use the best ingredients. Tough tasteless meat or mealy tomatoes will not improve with cooking. They will ruin your dish.

Soups & Starters

Cheddar Potato Soup	18
Chilled Golden Beet & Fennel Soup	20
Foie Gras Brulee	21
French Onion Soup	22
Garlic Escargot w/ Kasseri Cheese	23
Ginger Garlic Chicken Soup	24
Mexican Cheese & Chicken Dip	26
Mussels in Lemon Grass Curry Coconut Broth	27
Pepper Jack Ham and Cauliflower Soup	29
Pineapple Mango Duck Nachos	30
Pizzaola Hamburger Sliders	31
Polenta Crackers with Sausage & Meatballs	32
Pork & Shrimp Dumplings	34
South of the Border Shrimp & Sausage Soup	36
Spicy Black Bean Soup	37
Spinach & Artichoke Dip	38
Vichyssoise	39

Cheddar Potato Soup

- Serves: 6.
- Preparation time is 20 minutes.
- Cooking time is 2 hours.

Ingredients

    4 medium yukon gold potatoes, finely chopped
    3 medium leeks, thinly sliced
    2 cups chicken stock
  1/2 can light beer
    2 bay leaves
1 1/2 teaspoons mustard powder
1 1/2 teaspoons garlic powder
    2 cups cheddar cheese, shredded
    4 ounces low fat cream cheese
    5 16 ounce ramekins
    4 pieces bacon, cooked
      cheddar cheese, shredded, for garnish

Instructions

Heat a water bath to 189°

Clean the leeks by leaving the root end on and slice in half lengthwise. Place in a bowl of water and spread the layers of the leak out so that the water will be able to clean the layers. Drain and pat dry. Cut the leeks by leaving the root end on and slicing lengthwise into 3 sections. Cut across the width to slice the leeks thinly. Discard the root end. Place the leeks into a mixing bowl with a spout.

Combine the chicken stock, beer, bay leaves, mustard, and garlic powder in a sauce pan. Bring to a boil and reduce to a simmer for about 10 mins. Remove from heat and remove the bay leaves. Allow to cool a little. Add the cream cheese and the cheddar cheese. If the consistency of the cheese is not melting, use an immersion blender to smooth into a sauce or place in a blender. Pour the mixture over the leeks and place in the refrigerator to cool.

Peel and dice the potatoes into 1/4 inch cubes. Equally divide among the 16 ounce ramekins. Pour the leek soup mixture into the ramekins and mix with the potatoes. Place each ramekin into individual bags.

Pulse to seal- do not worry if the liquid begins to pour into the bag as you will be dividing the soup among other bowls to serve. Place ramekins in the water bath for two hours. * Remove from bags and serve in preheated bowls. Garnish with cooked bacon and shredded cheddar cheese.

Recipe Notes

WARNING THIS RECIPE CONTAINS ALCOHOL.

*Preheat your bowls either in an oven or pour boiling water in bowls right before serving. This will allow the soup to retain its warm temperature. By cooking the potatoes sous vide you are retaining all of the minerals and nutrition. Your soup will not overcook.

Chilled Golden Beet & Fennel Soup

- Serves: 4.
- Preparation time is 20 minutes.
- Inactive preparation time is 20 minutes.
- Cooking time is 2 hours.

Ingredients

2 large golden beets, peeled & diced into 1/2 cubes
1 medium fennel bulb, cored & sliced
1/2 cup chicken stock
2 teaspoons thyme
1 teaspoon ginger
1 9 x 5 metal loaf pan
1 teaspoon salt
1 large orange, juiced
1 1/2 teaspoons cinnamon
1 tablespoon sour cream
2 cups chicken stock

Instructions

Heat a water bath to 185°.

Place the beets into a loaf pan. Add the fennel, thyme and ginger, and the 1/2 cup of chicken stock and mix well. Place the loaf pan in a bag and pulse to seal. Cook for two hours.

Remove loaf pan from bag and allow to cool. Place cooled vegetables in a food processor and process until smooth. Add the juice of the orange, salt and cinnamon and process. Add the sour cream and process until well incorporated. Pour into a container and place in the refrigerator. Allow the soup to chill for at least four hours.

Foie Gras Brulee

- Serves: 4.
- Preparation time is 10 minutes.
- Cooking time is 2 hours.

Ingredients

    1 cup heavy cream
    4 egg yolks
    6 ounces foie gras with black truffles
    2 cups balsamic vinegar
    4 tablespoons brown sugar
1/2 pint blackberries
    4 6 ounce ramekins
    1 tablespoon kosher salt, for sprinkling
    1 teaspoon ground black pepper, for sprinkling

Instructions

Preheat a water bath to 165°.

Blend the eggs, cream, and foie gras in a blender or food processor. Pour mixture into the ramekins. Place ramekins in individual bags and pulse to seal. Place in water bath for a minimum of two hours.

Make the balsamic drizzle. Bring the balsamic vinegar and brown sugar to a boil in a small saucepan. Reduce heat to a simmer and cook until liquid is reduced by half (about 10 minutes). Remove from heat and cool. Place the foie gras ramekins on a small plate. Drizzle the balsamic reduction on top and sprinkle with the kosher salt and pepper. Top with berries. Serve and enjoy.

Recipe Notes

D'Artagnan's foie gras with black truffles was used in this recipe.

French Onion Soup

- Serves: 3.
- Preparation time is 10 minutes.
- Inactive preparation time is 10 minutes.
- Cooking time is 2 hours.

<u>Ingredients</u>

      4 cups beef broth
      1 tablespoon Worcestershire sauce
1 1/2 teaspoons thyme
1 1/2 teaspoons dijon mustard
  1/4 cup dry sherry
    2 tablespoons butter
    1 large onion, thinly sliced
    3 10 ounce stoneware crocks
    1 baguette, sliced 1/2" thick
    6 slices Gruyere

<u>Instructions</u>

Heat a water bath to 185°.

Slice the onion and place in a bag with the butter. Remove air and seal. Place in the water bath and cook for two hours.

Make the broth fifteen minutes before the onions are ready. Add the dry sherry to a sauce pan and cook over medium heat. Reduce down by half. Add the beef broth, Worcestershire sauce, thyme and dijon. Lower the heat and cover with a lid until ready to serve.

Preheat the broiler 10 minutes before ready to serve. Remove the onions from the bag (snip off a corner of the bag to allow the butter to drain out) and mix the onions into the broth. Pour soup into crocks. Place the crocks on a baking sheet. Slice three pieces of the baguette. Top each crock with a 1" thick baguette slice and top with two slices each Gruyere cheese. Place under the broiler and broil until cheese is golden and bubbly. Serve.

<u>Recipe Notes</u>

WARNING THIS RECIPE CONTAINS ALCOHOL.

Garlic Escargot w/ Kasseri Cheese

- Serves: 4.
- Preparation time is 10 minutes.
- Cooking time is 4 hours.

Ingredients

12	ounces Kasseri cheese, sliced
8 1/2	ounces escargot
1/2	cup minced garlic
1/2	cup butter
24	creminni mushroom caps, stems removed
4	escargot dishes

Instructions

Heat a water bath to 180°.

Brown the mushrooms in the butter over high heat. Remove from skillet and cool.

Drain and rinse the escargot. Pat dry. Place the escargots in a escargot dish. *Place 1 tsp.of minced garlic each on top of the escargots followed by the 1 tsp. butter. Top with the creminni mushroom caps. Place the sliced cheese on top of the mushrooms. Place the escargot dishes in an individual bag and pulse to seal. Place in the water bath and cook for a minimum of 4 hours.

Recipe Notes

* Use the minced garlic that is in a jar for this recipe or roast the garlic ahead of time. If you use fresh garlic it will have a bitter taste.

Ginger Garlic Chicken Soup

- Serves: 4.
- Preparation time is 20 minutes.
- Cooking time is 3 hours.

Ingredients

16	ounces baby carrots, chopped in 1/2
4	medium leeks, thinly sliced
1	stalk celery, finely diced
1	small onion, finely diced
1/2	cup frozen peas
1	large chicken breast, boneless & skinless, cut in chunks
5	ounces fettuccine, broken up
2	tablespoons fresh ginger, grated
1	tablespoon garlic, minced
2	bay leaves
6	cups chicken stock
5	tablespoons margarine
1	teaspoon garlic powder
1	teaspoon ground ginger
1 1/2	tablespoons olive oil

Instructions

Heat a water bath to 185°.

Place the carrots and leeks in a bag with 4 tbls. margarine. Remove the air and seal. Place in the water bath for 2 hours.

* Lower the water bath to 151° after the carrots and leaks have finished cooking. They will remain in the water bath with the chicken and will not continue to cook. Cut the chicken into one inch size chunks and season with the 1 tsp. garlic powder and 1 tsp. ground ginger. Place the chicken pieces in a bag and add 1 tbls. margarine. Remove the air and seal. Cook for 1 hour.

Saute the onions and celery over medium heat in olive oil until soft and translucent. Add the minced garlic and grated ginger and cook for 2 minutes. Add the chicken stock and the bay leaves. Bring up to a boil and add the broken fettuccine noodles. Slightly under cook the pasta according to package times and reduce down to a simmer. Do this 20 minutes before the chicken has finished cooking in the water bath.

Remove the chicken and the vegetables from the bags and add to the chicken stock. Stir in the frozen peas. Serve.

Recipe Notes

*If you have two water ovens, you will be able to cook the chicken and the vegetables simultaneously.

Mexican Cheese & Chicken Dip

- Serves: 6.
- Preparation time is 5 minutes.
- Cooking time is 3 hours.

Ingredients

2 boneless skinless chicken breasts
2 tablespoons ancho chili powder
1 tablespoon garlic powder
4 tablespoons butter
1 cup mayonnaise
1 tablespoon cumin
1/2 cup sour cream
1 1/2 tablespoons lime juice
2 tablespoons hot sauce
15 ounces black beans, rinsed & drained
2 bunches scallions, finely chopped
1 package frozen corn, thawed
4 medium tomatoes, chopped
2 cups Mexican blend cheese, shredded
1 bunch cilantro, finely chopped
1 package blue corn tortilla chips

Instructions

Heat a water bath to 150°.

Sprinkle the ancho chili powder, cumin, and garlic powder on both sides of chicken breasts. Place in a bag and top with butter. Remove the air and seal. Place in water bath for 3 hours. Open the bag and pour the au jus into a large mixing bowl. Chop the chicken into small pieces.

Add the mayonnaise, sour cream, hot sauce and lime juice to the mixing bowl containing the au jus. Stir well. Add the chicken and the six remaining ingredients. Refrigerate for at least one hour. Serve with blue corn tortilla chips.

Mussels in Lemon Grass Curry Coconut Broth

- Serves: 4.
- Preparation time is 5 minutes.
- Cooking time is 40 minutes.

<u>Ingredients</u>

```
    4  cups vegetable broth
    7  ounces light coconut milk
2 1/2  tablespoons curry powder
    1  teaspoon garlic paste
    1  teaspoon pesto paste
    6  stalks lemon grass, thinly sliced
    3  pounds frozen mussels in garlic butter
    1  bunch chives, finely chopped
    1  bunch cilantro, finely chopped
    2  9 x 5 metal loaf pans
```

<u>Instructions</u>

Heat a water bath to 140°.

Divide the frozen mussels into the two loaf pans. Place each loaf pan into an individual large bag. Pulse to seal. *Place in the water bath. Place plates on top to submerge the pans. Cook for 40 minutes.

Cook the lemon grass with the vegetable broth in a sauce pan over medium heat. Add the curry powder. Bring to a boil. Cook for 2 minutes and reduce the heat to medium low. Cover the sauce pan with a lid and simmer for 20 minutes. Remove the sauce pan from heat and strain the soup mixture through a sieve into another sauce pan. Discard the lemon grass. Place the sauce pan back on the stove and add the garlic paste and the pesto paste. Cook over medium heat for about another two minutes. Stir until well incorporated. Add the coconut milk. Keep warm until ready to serve.

Remove the mussels from the pans and equally divide into portions. Spoon the broth over the mussels. Top with the cilantro and the chives. Serve.

Recipe Notes

*Mussels that are frozen are precooked and pasteurized.

Pepper Jack Ham & Cauliflower Soup

- Serves: 4.
- Preparation time is 10 minutes.
- Cooking time is 2 hours.

Ingredients

1/2 head cauliflower
1 large leek, thinly sliced/white part only
1 medium yukon gold potato, 1/2 inch cubes
3 tablespoons margarine
5 cups chicken stock
1/2 cup heavy cream
4 ounces low fat cream cheese
12 ounces ham, cubed
16 ounces pepper jack cheese, shredded

Instructions

Heat a water bath to 185°.

Cut the cauliflower flowerettes into bite size pieces. Clean and slice the leeks horizontally. Peel and chop the yukon gold into 1/2 inch cubes. Place the vegetables into a bag and top with the margarine. Remove the air and seal. Place in the water bath for 2 hours.

Heat the stock on top of the stove over medium heat. Add the cream. Remove the vegetables from the bath and place half of the vegetables and the liquid from the bag into the stock. Using a hand blender, puree the vegetables or process in a food processor or blender. When the broth is warmed through, lower the heat and stir in the cream cheese and the pepper jack cheese. Add the ham and the remaining vegetables and continue to heat on low until thoroughly warmed through. Serve.

Recipe Notes

This is a spicy soup. If you prefer less heat add only half of the pepper jack cheese to the broth.

Pineapple Mango Duck Nachos

- Serves: 4.
- Preparation time is 15 minutes.
- Cooking time is 1 hour.

Ingredients

> 1 1/2 duck, precooked
> 1 can pinto beans, rinsed
> 1 bunch scallions, finely chopped
> 1 bunch cilantro leaves, finely chopped
> 3 cups 4 Mexican Cheese Blend
> 5 ounces blue corn tortilla chips
> 1 jar Pace Pineaspple Mango Chipolte Salsa

Instructions

Heat a water bath to 150°.

Place the *1/2 duck in a bag. Remove the air and seal. Place in the water bath and cook for 1 hour if frozen or 1/2 an hour if thawed. **
Place the rinsed beans in a separate bag. Remove the air and seal.
Place in the water bath with the duck.

Preheat the broiler. Place the blue corn tortilla chips on an aluminum foil lined baking sheet. Top with cheese. Place under broiler and melt the cheese.

Remove the duck from the bag. Remove the skin. Shred the meat with a fork. Top the nachos with the pinto beans and the shredded duck. Sprinkle the cilantro and scallions on top. Serve the pineapple mango chipotle salsa on the side. Serve and enjoy.

Recipe Notes

*Pre cooked duck from Maple Leaf Farms was used in this recipe.

**Use canned pinto beans. The water bath will warm the beans but the beans are already cooked.

Pizzaola Hamburger Sliders

- Serves: 12.
- Preparation time is 20 minutes.
- Cooking time is 1 hour.

<u>Ingredients</u>

2	pounds ground beef
2	tablespoons minced onion
3/4	pound wild mushrooms, finely chopped
4	ounces sun-dried tomatoes in oil, finely chopped
3/4	pound pepperoni, finely chopped
2	tablespoons basil
2	tablespoons oregano
1 1/3	tablespoons fennel seeds
12	small bocconcini mozzarella
12	mini hamburger buns

<u>Instructions</u>

Heat a water bath to 150°.

Pat dry the sun-dried tomatoes to remove the excess oil. Combine the meat with the other ingredients in a mixing bowl with the exception of the bocconcini and hamburger buns. Mix well until everything is well incorporated.

Spread meat mixture onto a piece of aluminum foil or wax paper. Pat out meat mixture until it is about 1/4 inch thick. Using a table knife score into 2 inch squares. Pick up one square of meat and place one bocconcini in the middle. Top with another square of meat and enclose the cheese. Repeat the process. Place the mini burgers in a bag leaving space between each burger and pulse to seal. If you over pulse the burgers will flatten. Place in a water bath for 1 hour. Remove and place on mini hamburger buns. Top with your favorite garnishes such as pesto sauce, tomato pesto, garlic mayonnaise with olives, etc.

Polenta Crackers with Sausage & Meatballs

- Serves: 6.
- Preparation time is 10 minutes.
- Inactive preparation time is 10 minutes.
- Cooking time is 30 minutes.

Ingredients

1	cup polenta, cooked
2	chicken sausages w/feta & spinach, cut 1" thick pieces
6	chicken meatballs, see recipe
2	Italian sausage with tomato & mozzarella
1	tube of of black olive paste
1	tube of pesto paste
1	small onion, sliced
1	jar sun-dried tomatoes in oil
1/2	cup Parmesan cheese, grated
1	tablespoon olive oil, for sauteing

Instructions

Heat a water bath to 150°.

Cut the sausages up. Place each type of sausage in an individual bag. Remove the air and seal. Prepare the meatballs ahead of time (see recipe). Place the pre-cooked meatballs in an individual bag. Pulse to seal. Do not over pulse or the meatballs will be crushed. Place the bags in the water bath and cook for a minimum of 1/2 hour to reheat.

Prepare the polenta (see recipe). Pour the cooked polenta onto a parchment paper lined baking sheet. Spread the mixture very thin about 1/4 inch. Place in the refrigerator to cool and set.

Preheat a griddle to 400°. Using a biscuit cutter, cut the polenta into 2 inch rounds. Place on the griddle and cook on both sides until browned. * Place in a low oven (185°) on a wire mesh rack or a pizza stone.

Heat the olive oil over medium high heat. Add the sliced onions and cook until carmelized.

Pat dry approximately 10 sun-dried tomatoes and cut into slices. When ready to serve the polenta crackers, top each with grated parmesan, slices of onion and sun-dried tomato strips. Remove the sausages and meatballs from the water oven. Squeeze pesto sauce on 1/3 of the crackers and top with the meatballs. Squeeze the olive paste onto the other 1/3 and top with the Italian sausage. Top the remaining crackers with the chicken feta/spinach sausages.

Recipe Notes

*Placing the polenta on a pizza stone or a wire mesh screen which is used for dehydrating vegetables and or fruits, will keep them from getting soggy. You may top them with the onions and sun-dried tomatoes while you are waiting for the sausages and meatballs to cook.

Pork & Shrimp Dumplings

- Serves: 6.
- Preparation time is 10 minutes.
- Inactive preparation time is 10 minutes.
- Cooking time is 1 1/2 hours.

Ingredients

   1 pound ground pork
   6 ounces shrimp, peeled & chopped
   8 ounces shitake mushrooms, minced
   1 tablespoon grapeseed oil, for sauteing
   4 scallions, finely diced
   4 ounces water chestnuts, finely diced
   2 tablespoons sesame oil
   2 tablespoons dry sherry
   2 teaspoons ginger
   6 rice wrappers, 6 inch diameter
 36 cilantro leaves
     Sauce
1/4 cup rice wine vinegar
   3 tablespoons ketchup
   1 tablespoon brown sugar
   2 tablespoons Worcestershire sauce

Instructions

Heat a water bath to 143°.

Saute the shitake mushrooms in the grapeseed oil over high heat until browned. Remove from heat and let cool.

In a mixing bowl, combine the pork, scallions, shrimp, ginger, sherry, diced water chestnuts, and sesame oil. Finely chop the cooled mushrooms and add to the mixture. Stir to incorporate. Place the mixture into a bag in a layer that is about 1/2 inch thick. Pulse to seal and place in the water bath. Cook for 1 1/2 hours.

*Remove the pork mixture from bath. Lower the water bath to 128°. Slit one corner of the bag to allow the liquid to drain out. Open the bag and let the pork mixture cool. Pour very warm water into a pie plate. Wet a towel and place on the counter top. One at a time, place a rice wrapper in the hot water. It should completely soften. Place the softened rice wrapper on the wet towel. Place six cilantro leaves down the middle of the rice wrapper. Spoon some of the pork mixture onto the rice wrapper. Fold the top edge of the rice wrapper over the meat mixture and then the sides of the wrapper. Gently roll to enclose. Repeat the process until all of the filling has been used. Put the rolled pork dumplings into a bag, allowing space between them so that they will not get stuck together when sealing. Pulse to seal. Place in the water bath to keep warm until ready to serve. Do not keep in the water bath longer than 30 minutes as the rice wrapper tends to get too soft.

Make the dipping sauce by combining the ketchup, rice wine vinegar, brown sugar and Worcestershire sauce. Leave out at room temperature. Remove the dumplings from the bag and plate to serve.

Recipe Notes

WARNING THIS RECIPE CONTAINS ALCOHOL WHICH HAS NOT BEEN COOKED OUT.

*You may cook the pork mixture the day before. Place in an ice bath for 1 hour after it has finished cooking. Refrigerate. You may also place the cooled pork mixture into the rice wrappers and place in a bag. Reheat in a 128° water bath.

South of the Border Shrimp and Sausage Soup

- Serves: 4.
- Preparation time is 10 minutes.
- Cooking time is 30 minutes.

Ingredients

    1/2 pound shrimp, peeled
      4 andouille sausages, cut into bite size pieces
         Mexican rice (see recipe)
      6 cups chicken stock
      2 cups corn nachos, crumbled
      4 tablespoons sour cream, for garnish
      2 bunches scallions, thinly sliced
      1 cup extra sharp cheddar cheese, shredded

Instructions

Heat a water bath to 143°.

If the shrimp are large, cut into bite size pieces. Put the shrimp and sausage into a bag. Remove the air and seal. Cook for 30 minutes.

*Meanwhile prepare the rice according to the recipe but eliminating the scallions and cheddar cheese. This will be added to the soup to garnish. Add the chicken stock to the finished rice. Heat the stock over low.

Add the cooked shrimp/sausage to the chicken stock and rice mixture. Pour into bowls and garnish with the crushed nacho chips. sour cream and scallions.

Recipe Notes

*You may prepare the Mexican rice recipe ahead of time. It will keep in the refrigerator for a couple of days.

Spicy Black Bean Soup

- Serves: 2.
- Preparation time is 5 minutes.
- Cooking time is 3 hours.

Ingredients

   1 cup salsa
15 ounces black beans
   1 cup chicken stock
      sour cream, for garnish
      sharp cheddar cheese, to taste
   4 scallions, finely chopped
   4 ounces andouille sausages, 1/4 inch dice
   2 16 ounce ramekins

Instructions

Heat a water bath to 165 °.

Cut the sausage into 1/4 inch dice. Divide the portions of sausage equally among the ramekins. Drain and rinse the black beans. Divide the beans equally among the ramekins. Divide the salsa (prepared jar of salsa or your own) and mix into the bean/sausage mixture. Add the chicken stock. Place the ramekins in individual bags. Pulse to seal. If some of the liquid flows outside of the ramekin do not worry. Upon removing the ramekins from the bag, carefully save the liquid which has accumulated inside the bag and incorporate back into the soup. Place in water bath and cook for 3 hours.

Remove the ramekins from the bags and using an immersion blender gently pulse in the ramekin until the soup is thickened. Top with cheese, sour cream, and scallions. Enjoy.

Spinach Artichoke Dip

- Serves: 6.
- Preparation time is 10 minutes.
- Cooking time is 30 minutes.

Ingredients

```
12  ounces fresh spinach
28  ounces artichoke hearts
 8  ounces low fat cream cheese
 1  tablespoon garlic, minced
 3  tablespoons mayonnaise
 1  dash hot sauce
1/2 cup Parmesan cheese, grated
1/2 cup Asiago cheese, grated
 1  16 ounce ramekin
```

Instructions

Heat a water bath to 172°.

In a food processor, puree the spinach followed by the artichokes. Add the cream cheese and the mayonnaise. Process until smooth. Add the *minced garlic, hot sauce, and cheeses. Pour into ramekin and place in a bag. Pulse to seal. Place in a water bath and cook for minimum of 30 minutes.

Serve with corn tortilla chips or spoon on top of cooked chicken breasts.

Recipe Notes

*Use minced garlic in a jar. Do not use raw minced garlic.

Vichyssoise

- Serves: 8.
- Preparation time is 10 minutes.
- Cooking time is 2 hours.

Ingredients

   10 yukon gold potatoes, thinly sliced
    6 large leeks, white part only, thinly sliced
    2 large onions, chopped
   10 cups chicken stock
    1 teaspoon marjoram, dried
 1/2 tablespoon thyme
    2 bay leaves
1 1/2 cups heavy cream
    5 tablespoons butter

Instructions

Heat a water bath to 185°.

Thoroughly clean the leeks and pat dry. Divide the sliced potatoes, leeks, and onions into two bags with the butter. Remove the air and seal. Place in the water bath and cook for two hours.

Heat the chicken stock, marjoram, thyme and bay leaves in a saucepan. Cover with a lid and simmer for 30 minutes. Remove lid and allow to cool. Remove the two bay leaves.

*Remove the potato mixture from the water bath and pour contents into the sauce pan containing the chicken stock. Using an immersion blender, process until smooth. Refrigerate for a minimum of 4 hours before serving.

Serve by pouring the heavy cream equally divided among bowls. Ladle the soup into the bowls and mix well to incorporate the cream with the soup.

Recipe Notes

*Add the potato vegetable mixture a little at a time to the chicken stock and process. You may pour everything into a food processor & puree.

Brunch

Apricot Stuffed French Toast 41
Breakfast Strata 42
Carmel Apple Walnut Topping for Pancakes 44
Eggs Two Ways 45
Fiesta Rice Egg Cups with Jumbo Lump Crab 46
French Toast with Creme Brulee Sauce 48
Huevos Rancheros 50
Italian Frittata 51
Macaroni & Cheese Beef Hash with Eggs 53
Parmesan Baskets with Savory Tomato Egg Cups 55
Raspberry Coffee Cake 57

Apricot Stuffed French Toast

- Serves: 4.
- Preparation time is 10 minutes.
- Cooking time is 1 hour.

<u>Ingredients</u>

```
  8  pieces bread
  2  tablespoons margarine
  3  tablespoons apricot preserves
1/3  cup pecans, toasted
  2  eggs
1/2  teaspoon cinnamon
  1  tablespoon sugar
1/2  teaspoon vanilla extract
  4  ounces low fat cream cheese
  1  cup maple syrup, warmed
```

<u>Instructions</u>

Heat a water bath to 162 °.

Spread margarine on one side of each piece of bread. Place bread slices buttered side up on a baking sheet and toast under broiler until lightly browned. Remove from broiler and cool.

Mix the cream cheese together with the apricot preserves. Spread mixture on one piece of bread (untoasted side) and top with another piece of bread toasted side up. Repeat with remaining bread slices.

In another bowl, whisk the eggs with the cinnamon, vanilla, and sugar. Dip bread sandwiches in egg mixture and place into an individual bag. Pulse to seal. Place bags in the water bath and cook for a minimum of 1 hour.   Preheat a regular oven to 170°. Place serving plates in the oven to keep warm. Toast the pecans on top of the stove in a small skillet. Remove the french toast from bags and place on heated plates. Top with the toasted pecans. Drizzle warmed maple syrup on top. Serve.

Breakfast Strata

- Serves: 4.
- Preparation time is 20 minutes.
- Inactive preparation time is 20 minutes.
- Cooking time is 3 hours.

Ingredients

   10 ounces bread, cubed
    1 small onion, chopped
    6 ounces wild mushrooms, sliced
1 1/2 tablespoons butter, for sauteing
    4 ounces green chilies, diced
    4 ounces sun-dried tomatoes, thinly sliced
    2 cups extra sharp cheddar cheese, shredded
    4 eggs
    1 cup heavy cream
    2 teaspoons minced onion
    1 teaspoon dry mustard
1 1/2 teaspoons chicken flavored broth powder
    8 ounces ham, cubed
    6 slices extra sharp cheddar cheese, 4"x4"
    1 9 x 5 metal loaf pan

Instructions

Heat a water bath to 165°.

Preheat an oven to 200°. Place the cubed bread on a baking sheet and place in the oven for 20 to 30 minutes until bread is dry. Allow bread to cool.

Saute the mushrooms in the butter over high heat until they have browned. Add the onions and saute until they are translucent. Remove from heat and allow to cool.

In a food processor, add the eggs, heavy cream, mustard, minced onion, chicken flavored powder and shredded cheddar cheese. Process until smooth.

Using a large mixing bowl, combine the bread with the mushroom onion mixture, ham, green chilies and sun-dried tomatoes. Pour the egg mixture over the bread vegetable mixture and stir until everything is combined and the egg has coated the dry ingredients completely. *Pour into the loaf pan. Top the strata with the cheddar slices. Place the loaf pan in a bag and pulse to seal. The bag should be putting light pressure on top of the mixture. Place in the bath and cook for 3 hours.

Recipe Notes

*You may elect to cook the strata in individual ramekins instead of the loaf pan.

Frontier chicken broth powder was used in this recipe.

Carmel Apple Walnut Topping for Pancakes

- Serves: 4.
- Preparation time is 15 minutes.
- Cooking time is 40 minutes.

Ingredients

  2 pounds granny smith apples, peeled and cored
 12 ounces fat free carmel topping
  1 tablespoon cinnamon
 1/2 cup walnuts, chopped and roasted
  1 pinch xanthan gum, for thickening
  1 cup container of whipped cream topping, for garnish

Instructions

Heat a water bath to 185°.

Cut the apples into 1/2 inch slices. Place in a bag and sprinkle with cinnamon. Pour the contents of the carmel sauce into the bag. Mix well making sure the apples are all coated with the sauce. Pulse to seal and place in the bath. Weight down with plates to keep submerged.

Remove bag from bath. Cut off one small corner of bag and allow the liquid to drain out into a mixing bowl. Reseal the corner of the bag with the machine (it is not necessary to remove the air) and place apples back in bath to keep warm.

Pour the sauce into a food processor. *Add the xanthan gum to the liquid while the processor is running. Continue processing until thickened. Remove the warm apples from the bag and combine with thickened sauce. Top pancakes with apple carmel sauce and sprinkle with roasted walnuts. Garnish with whipped cream.

Recipe Notes

*The food processor must be running in order for the xanthan gum not to clump.

Eggs Two Ways

- Serves: 3.
- Cooking time is 2 hours.

Ingredients

      6 eggs
      6 16 ounce ramekins
      3 tablespoons butter, for garnish

Instructions

Heat a water bath to 148°.

Poach eggs by placing in the water bath for 1 hour. Crack open the shell and pour unto a slotted spoon. The uncooked white will drain through the spoon and be discarded. To cook a soft boiled egg, leave in the water bath for 2 hours. Serve.

An alternative way to cook the eggs is to crack the raw egg into a ramekin which contains 1/2 tbls. butter. Place each ramekin in an individual bag. Pulse to seal. The bag should just begin to put light pressure down upon the yolk. If too much pressure occurs the yolk will break. Place in a water bath and cook for the same amount of time as above.

Recipe Notes

This is a quicker way to cook and serve when you have a large group of people.

Fiesta Rice Egg Cups w/Jumbo Lump Crab

- Serves: 4.
- Preparation time is 20 minutes.
- Inactive preparation time is 20 minutes.
- Cooking time is 1 hour.

Ingredients

1	Family size brown rice in a bag
2	cups chicken stock
1	tablespoon Old Bay seasoning
1/2	large yellow bell pepper, finely chopped
1/2	large red bell pepper, finely chopped
1	celery stalk, finely chopped
1	bunch scallions, finely chopped
2	tablespoons butter, for sauteing
2	cups extra sharp cheddar cheese, shredded
2 1/2	tablespoons mayonnaise
1	bunch asparagus tips
6	medium tomatoes, sliced
32	ounces lump crab meat
4	4" dia. spring form pans

Sauce

1/2	teaspoon dijon mustard
1	tablespoon lemon juice
1/2	cup butter, melted
5	large eggs

Instructions

Heat a water bath to 148°.

Preheat an oven to 185°.

Prepare the rice according to package directions, replacing the water with the chicken broth and adding the Old Bay seasoning. Allow rice to cool. Saute the celery, scallions and peppers in the butter until softened. Remove from heat and allow to cool. Fold the pepper mixture into the rice. Add the mayonnaise and the cheese to the mixture and mix well.

46

Equally divide the rice mixture among the spring form pans, pressing the rice up the sides and bottom of the pan, and making a well for the egg. Crack an egg into each well. One egg will be reserved for the sauce. Place each pan in a separate bag. Pulse to seal, being careful that not too much pressure is placed on the egg yolk, as it will burst. Weight down with a plate to keep submerged. Place in the water bath for 1 hour.

Slice the tomatoes and place in a circle around the perimeter of the serving plates. Place in the oven.

Sous vide the asparagus (see recipe) 20 minutes before serving.

Make the sauce in a blender. Combine the eggs, lemon and dijon and process. Heat the butter in the microwave until melted. Pour the hot butter into the blender while it is running. It should thicken up right away. Keep sauce warm.

To plate, carefully remove the spring form pan from the rice/egg cups and place in the center of each plate (leave the bottom of the pan on). The tomatoes should be forming a circle around the rice/egg cups. Take the asparagus tips and cluster them between the tomatoes slices. Place the jumbo lump crab on top of the asparagus and tomatoes and drizzle the sauce on top. Serve.

French Toast with Creme Brulee Sauce

- Serves: 2.
- Preparation time is 10 minutes.
- Cooking time is 2 hours.

<u>Ingredients</u>

    4 pieces bread, toasted
    4 egg yolks
    3 tablespoons sugar
  1/4 teaspoon vanilla extract
1 1/2 cups heavy cream
    1 tablespoon brown sugar
  1/4 teaspoon butter
      cinnamon, for sprinkling
      sugar, for sprinkling
  1/4 cup walnuts, toasted
      carmel sauce, for drizzling
    2 16 ounce ramekins

<u>Instructions</u>

Heat a water bath to 165 °.

Toast the bread in a toaster. Butter the toast on one side of each piece of toast. Sprinkle the cinnamon and sugar on top of each buttered toast.

In a mixing bowl, whisk together the egg yolks, vanilla, white sugar, brown sugar, and heavy cream. Dip each piece of toast into the mixture, coating well. Place one piece of toast (cinnamon coated side down) into the bottom of each dish. Pour 1/2 of the cream/egg mixture on top of each toast. Place another piece of soaked toast (cinnamon side up) on top of the cream mixture.   Repeat the process with the remaining toast slices. If any of the cream mixture remains, pour it on top of the toast. Place each ramekin in an individual 11 inch wide bag. Allow enough length for sealing. Slowly pulse until light pressure begins to be placed on top of the egg mixture. Over pulsing will result in the egg mixture being sucked out of the ramekin and into the bag. Seal and carefully place in the water bath. Try not to tip the ramekin or the liquid will flow out of the ramekin. Cook for a minimum of two hours.

Just before plating, toast the walnuts in a small skillet. Heat the carmel sauce. Remove ramekins from the bags and place on a serving plate. Drizzle carmel sauce on top of the french toast and top with the toasted walnuts

Huevos Rancheros

- Serves: 4.
- Preparation time is 5 minutes.
- Cooking time is 1 hour.

Ingredients

    8 eggs
10 ounces black beans, drained & rinsed
16 ounces salsa, drained
  2 cups Mexican blend cheese, shredded
  4 6" round dishes
  4 flour tortillas

Instructions

Heat a water bath to 148°.

Rinse and drain the beans. Slightly mash the black beans. Pour the salsa into a fine mesh strainer. Allow the liquid to drain out. Combine the beans with the salsa in a bowl. Divide the mixture evenly into the dishes. Top each dish with the cheese. Place in an individual bag and pulse to seal. Place in the water bath. Place the eggs (in their shells) on top of the dishes. Cook for one hour. Do not overcook or the eggs will not be poached and will become hard.

Keep the * tortillas warm in a oven.

Carefully remove the eggs. Remove dishes from bags and place on top of serving plates. Crack one egg at a time over a bowl into a slotted spoon. The excess white which has not set up will drop through the spoon and will be discarded. Top the bean mixture with the egg. Repeat the process, topping each bean dish with two eggs each. Serve with salsa and the warmed tortillas.

Recipe Notes

*Blue corn tortilla chips are also a nice accompaniment in place of the tortillas.

Italian Frittata

- Serves: 6.
- Preparation time is 10 minutes.
- Inactive preparation time is 10 minutes.
- Cooking time is 2 hours and 40 minutes.

<u>Ingredients</u>

```
   12  eggs
    2  tablespoons sour cream
    2  teaspoons oregano
    2  teaspoons basil
  1/2  cup Parmesan cheese, grated
    1  tablespoon minced onion
   10  slices pepperoni, 2" diameter
    1  hot Italian sausage
    6  ounces mushrooms thinly sliced
    1  small onion, chopped
    1  tablespoon butter, for sauteing
    5  slices round provolone cheese slices
  1/4  cup chunky marinara sauce
    3  tablespoons basil, chiffonade
  1/4  cup Parmesan cheese, grated, for garnish
    1  6" spring form pan
```

<u>Instructions</u>

Heat a water bath to 165°.

In a mixing bowl, crack the 12 eggs and add the sour cream. Whisk the eggs for 5 minutes until the sour cream is completely incorporated and the eggs are fluffy. Add the basil, oregano, minced onion and the Parmesan. Mix well. Pour the mixture into the 6" spring form pan. Place in a bag and pulse to seal. The top of the bag should be putting pressure on top of the egg mixture. Place in the bath and cook for 2 hours.

After two hours lower the water bath to 150°.

Saute the mushrooms over medium high heat in butter until browned. Lower the heat to medium and add the onions. Saute until translucent. Remove from skillet and allow to cool. Using a salad plate, place the pepperoni in a circle form. The pepperoni will be placed on top of the frittata. Try to maintain the size (diameter) to match the size of the frittata. Next, break up the sausage and place on top the pepperoni. Put the onion mushroom mixture on top followed by the provolone slices. Place the plate inside a bag and seal. Place in the 150° water bath. Cook for 30 minutes.

Heat the marinara sauce in a small sauce pan over low heat. Remove the spring form pan from the bag and place inverted onto a large serving platter. Remove the sides of the pan and gently pry off the bottom with a knife. Remove the pepperoni circle from the bag and invert on top of the top of the frittata. The pepperoni should now be on top. Spoon the warm marinara sauce on top. Sprinkle with the 1/4 cup of parmesan and top with the basil.

Macaroni & Cheese Beef Hash with Eggs

- Serves: 4.
- Preparation time is 15 minutes.
- Inactive preparation time is 15 minutes.
- Cooking time is 3 hours.

Ingredients

         4 medium yukon gold potatoes, cubed
         2 tablespoons butter
         6 ounces low fat cream cheese
       1/2 cup beef broth
         1 tablespoon minced onion
         1 teaspoon dry mustard
         1 cup extra sharp cheddar cheese, shredded
     4 1/2 ounces dried beef, shredded
         4 eggs
        10 ounces elbow macaroni, cooked
         4 16 ounce ramekins

Instructions

Heat a water bath to 185°.

Peel and cut the potatoes into 1/4 inch cubes. Place in a bag with the 2 tbls. butter. Remove the air and seal. Place in the water bath for two hours. Drain liquid from bag by cutting off a corner of the bag. Open bag and pour potatoes into a bowl. Allow to cool. When potatoes have cooled, combine the dried beef with the potatoes.

Lower the water bath to 148°.

Meanwhile, cook the macaroni according to package directions. Allow the macaroni to cool.

To make the sauce for the macaroni, place the cream cheese, cheddar cheese, beef broth, minced onion and dry mustard in a blender. Process until smooth. Mixture should not be runny. It should be some what thick like wall paper paste.

Combine the sauce with the macaroni and mix well. Divide the macaroni equally between the ramekins. Next, top with the beef and potato mixture leaving a well or indentation in the middle. Place an egg in each well. Place each ramekin in an individual bag and pulse to seal. Gentle pressure of the bag should be touching the top of the egg. Over pulsing will cause the egg to break. Place in the bath and cook for 1 hour. Remove from bags and serve.

Parmesan Baskets w/ Savoury Tomato Egg Cups

- Serves: 4.
- Preparation time is 10 minutes.
- Cooking time is 1 hour.

Ingredients

  1 cup Parmesan cheese, grated
  4 large tomatoes
12 spinach leaves, blanched
  4 eggs
  1 tablespoon oregano
  1 tablespoon basil
  1 tablespoon garlic powder
  4 14 ounce ramekins
  4 slices bacon, cooked
  4 tablespoons pesto sauce

Instructions

Heat a water bath to 148°.

Preheat an oven to 350°.

Slice off the very top of the tomatoes. Using a small melon baller, carefully scoop out the seeds and pulp of tomato, leaving adequate thickness to support the egg. Save the seeds and pulp. Sprinkle the spices inside each tomato. Place each tomato into a 14 ounce ramekin (the sides of the ramekin should be taller than the tomato). Place three blanched spinach leaves inside each tomato, allowing the leaves to overlap and extend out of the tomato. Crack an egg into each tomato. Place the reserved pulp of the tomatoes in the bottom of the ramekins. Place the ramekins in individual bags. Pulse to seal, being careful not to over pulse, so that the yolk will not break. Place in the water bath and cook for 1 hour.

Use a silcon mat to make the Parmesan baskets. Sprinkle the Parmesan cheese into 5 inch rounds on the silcon mats. Place in the oven and cook for about 10 minutes or until rounds have turned golden brown. Remove from the oven. Using a spatula, remove the rounds and place on top of an inverted 3 inch diameter glass. Allow the sides of the rounds to loosely drape over the sides of the glass. Let

Parmesan rounds cool and harden. Remove from glass and place on a serving plate.

When eggs are ready, remove the tomato from ramekins and gently place inside the Parmesan baskets. Spoon reserved tomato pulp around the inside of the Parmesan basket. Garnish with the pesto sauce and a strip of bacon. Serve.

Raspberry Coffee Cake

- Serves: 4.
- Preparation time is 10 minutes.
- Inactive preparation time is 10 minutes.
- Cooking time is 2 hours.

<u>Ingredients</u>

      4 cups dried bread crumbs
      2 large eggs
    3/4 cup extra fine sugar
      1 teaspoon vanilla extract
      6 ounces raspberry cake/pastry filling
    1/2 cup walnuts, chopped
      6 tablespoons confectioners sugar
      1 tablespoon milk
    1/4 teaspoon raspberry liqueur
      4 cups 4 1/2 " dia. mini bundt pans

<u>Instructions</u>

Heat a water bath to 165°.

Preheat an oven to 200°.

Crumble bread into a food processor and process until fine. Place on a baking sheet and bake in a oven for 20 to 30 minutes until bread crumbs have dried and turned golden brown. Remove from oven and allow to cool.

Using a stand mixer, whisk the two eggs with the vanilla on high for 5 to 10 minutes, until the eggs have doubled in size and have become fluffy.

In a mixing bowl, combine the cooled bread crumbs with the sugar and mix well. Fold 1/3 of the egg mixture into the dry bread crumbs. Fold the remaining egg mixture into the bread crumbs. The mixture should resemble a cookie like consistency. It should not be overly moist like a cake batter. Pour the batter into each bundt pan 1/3 of the way up. Press down on the batter. * Spoon the raspberry pastry filling on top, followed by the remaining batter. Place each pan into a bag and pulse to seal. Place in the water bath and cook for 2 hours.

To make the icing, combine the raspberry liqueur with the confectioners sugar and the milk. Adjust the amount of milk to get the desired consistency for the icing. Toast the walnuts in a small skillet.

Remove the pans from the bags and allow to cool. Remove bundt pan and frost coffee cakes with icing. Top with roasted walnuts.

<u>Recipe Notes</u>

*Do not use pie filling for this recipe as it contains too much liquid.

Sandwiches & Burgers

Bison Burgers   60
Buffalo Chicken Burgers   61
Chicken Meatballs with Pimento Cheese Sauce   63
Chicken on Horseback   64
Chinese Chicken Lettuce Wraps   65
Greek Style Lamb Burgers   67
Gyros with Tzatziki Sauce   68
Patti Melt   70
Sante Fe Pork Tacos   71
Sirloin Burgers   72
Sloppy Joes   73

Bison Burgers

- Serves: 4.
- Preparation time is 15 minutes.
- Cooking time is 2 hours.

Ingredients

<u>Ingredients</u>

    1 pound bison meat, ground
    4 tablespoons margarine
    2 tablespoons grapeseed oil, for searing
    4 hamburger buns
       <u>Toppings</u>
    1 jar red pepper, drained
    1 small shallot, finely diced
  1/2 teaspoon lime juice
  1/2 teaspoon cumin
    1 tablespoon garlic, minced
  1/2 cup sour cream
    1 tablespoon chili powder
    1 avocado, mashed
  1/2 teaspoon cayenne pepper
    1 cup blue cheese, crumbled

Instructions

<u>Instructions</u>

Heat a water bath to 135°.

Divide the bison meat into four portions and form into 1 inch thick patties. Place patties on an aluminum foil lined baking sheet. Lightly coat each pattie with the grapeseed oil. Using a kitchen torch, sear the patties on all sides or heat a skillet over high heat. Add the grapeseed oil and sear patties quickly on both sides. Allow the patties to cool down. Place each pattie into an individual bag and top with 1 tbls. margarine. Remove the air by pulsing and seal. Place the bags in the water bath. Cook for a minimum of 2 hours.

For the toppings, mix together the mashed avocado, lime juice, cumin and minced garlic. Add the chili powder and cayenne to the sour cream. When the bison has cooked, remove from bags and place on the hamburger bun. Slice the red pepper into strips and place on top of the meat followed by the avocado mixture and the sour cream mixture. Sprinkle the crumbled blue cheese on top.

Buffalo Chicken Burgers

- Serves: 2.
- Preparation time is 15 minutes.
- Cooking time is 1 1/2 hours.

Ingredients

    1 pound chicken, ground
 1/2 cup celery, finely diced
 1/2 cup onion, finely chopped
      hot sauce, to taste
    3 tablespoons margarine
    3 cups fresh spinach
    1 bunch of scallions, thinly sliced
    2 hamburger buns
    6 slices bacon, cooked
    4 ounces low fat cream cheese
    2 tablespoons ranch dressing
 1/2 cup blue cheese, crumbled
    3 medium tomatoes, quartered

Instructions

Heat a water bath to 151°.

Saute the onion and celery in a tbls. of margarine until softened. Cool.
When the onion mixture has cooled, mix it into the chicken. Form 1
inch thick patties.

In a food processor, mix the remaining 2 tbls. of margarine and hot
sauce until well combined. Do not add too much hot sauce as you will
make the butter to thin. You can add more hot sauce at the end of
cooking.

Place each pattie in an individual bag and add 1 1/2 tbls. hot
sauce/margarine on top. Remove the air and seal. Place inthe water
bath. Cook for 1 1/2 hours.

To make the sauce, put the cream cheese in a food processor and slowly add the ranch dressing through the feed tube. You do not want the mixture to be to soupy. Pour into a serving bowl. Fold in the blue cheese crumbles.

Cook the bacon and chop the tomatoes. Place the baby spinach on a plate or place on top of a hamburger bun. Remove the chicken from the bags, reserving the sauce. Pour the sauce over the spinach, just enough to wilt and flavor. Put the chicken on top of the spinach and top with the blue cheese sauce. If you wish to have it a little hotter, pour more hot sauce on top of the blue cheese sauce. Top with the crumbled bacon, tomatoes, scallions, and the other half of the hamburger bun.

Chicken Meatballs w/ Pimento Cheese Sauce

- Serves: 4.
- Preparation time is 15 minutes.
- Cooking time is 1 hour.

Ingredients

1 pound ground chicken
6 scallions, finely chopped
6 slices bacon, crumbled
10 sun-dried tomatoes in oil, patted dry &chopped
2 teaspoons poultry seasoning
pimiento cheese (see recipe)
2 16 ounce ramekins
8 blue corn tortilla shells, warmed
4 tomatoes, chopped
1 cup lettuce

Instructions

Heat a water bath to 150°.

Combine the chicken with the scallions, sundried tomatoes (sliced into small pieces), crumbled bacon, and poultry seasoning. Using a small melon baller scoop up the chicken mixture and roll with your hands and shape into a meatball. *Place meatballs into a 16 ounce ramekin. Repeat this process. Place each ramekin into an individual bag and pulse to seal. You do not want too much pressure on top of the bag as it will compact the meatballs. Place in the water bath and cook for 1 hour.

Fill the blue corn tortillas with lettuce and tomatoes. Spoon pimento sauce on top. Place a couple of meatballs on top. Serve.

Recipe Notes

The cooking time is for 1 inch diameter meatballs.

*If you have mini muffin pans, you may cook the meatballs in these instead of the ramekins.

Chicken on Horseback

- Serves: 4.
- Preparation time is 15 minutes.
- Cooking time is 1 1/2 hours.

Ingredients

    4 chicken breasts, boneless & skinless
    4 andouille sausages, cut in 1/2 lenghtwise
  20 sun-dried tomatoes in oil, patted dry &chopped
    8 slices Provolone cheese
    4 bunches fresh basil, chiffonade
    4 tablespoons mayonnaise
    4 tablespoons dijon mustard
    4 tablespoons margarine
    8 slices sourdough bread

Instructions

Heat a water bath to 151°.

Make the spread topping by mixing the mayonnaise and dijon together.

Carefully butterfly the chicken breast. Place the chicken between two pieces of plastic wrap and pound out until thin. Be careful not to pound out too thin or holes will form. Remove wrap and place 1 slice of cheese folded in half on top of half of the chicken followed by one andouille sausage, sun dried tomatoes, basil and another piece of cheese folded in half. Fold the other half of the chicken over the sausage mixture. Try to completely enclose the mixture. Repeat this process with the remaining chicken breasts. Place the chicken in an individual bag with 1 tbls. margarine on top. Remove the air and seal. Place in the water bath and cook for 1 1/2 hours. When ready, remove and place on a slice of sourdough bread and top with the mayo/dijon spread and remaining slice of bread.

Recipe Notes

Cooking times are for 1/2 inch thick chicken breasts.

Chinese Chicken Lettuce Wraps

- Serves: 4.
- Preparation time is 15 minutes.
- Cooking time is 1 1/2 hours.

Ingredients

  1 1/2 pounds boneless skinless chicken breasts, cut into bite size
      pieces
    16 ounces shitake mushrooms, cleaned
     1 teaspoon ginger
     4 tablespoons soy sauce
  1 1/2 tablespoons water
     1 tablespoon dry sherry
     1 tablespoon chili-garlic sauce
     1 teaspoon sugar
     1 teaspoon sesame oil
     5 scallions, chopped
     8 ounces bamboo shoots, drained and chopped
     8 ounces water chestnuts, drained and chopped
     1 package chinese cellophane rice noodle, cooked to
      package directions
    10 iceburg lettuce leaves
     1 tablespoon grapeseed oil, for sauteing
     1 tablespoon garlic paste
      Sauce
     8 tablespoons soy sauce
     3 tablespoons water
     2 tablespoons dry sherry
     2 tablespoons chili-garlic sauce
     2 teaspoons sesame oil
     1 9 x 5 metal loaf pan

Instructions

Heat a water bath to 150°.

Saute the mushrooms in the grapeseed oil over high heat. Cook until
the mushrooms have browned. Remove from heat and allow to cool.
Chop up the mushrooms.

Combine the soy sauce, water, sherry, chili-garlic sauce, garlic paste, sugar and sesame oil. Stir to combine. Add the bite size chicken pieces, chopped scallions, bamboo shoots, and water chestnuts. Stir to coat everything well. Spoon mixture into the loaf pan. Place the pan in a large bag and pulse to seal. Place in a water bath and cook for 1 1/2 hours.

Make the sauce thirty minutes before serving. Combine the soy sauce, water, dry sherry, chili-garlic sauce and the sesame oil. The sauce may be prepared ahead of time and refrigerated. Allow the sauce to come to room temperature before serving. Toast the sesame seeds in a skillet.

Prepare the noodles and place on a platter. Spoon the chicken/vegetables on top of the noodles. Garnish with the toasted sesame seeds. Use the lettuce leaves like bread. Scoop up the rice noodles/chicken mixture and place inside the lettuce leaves. Spoon the sauce on top. Enjoy.

Recipe Notes

WARNING THIS RECIPE CONTAINS ALCOHOL.

You may substitute the iceberg lettuce for romaine lettuce. It doesn't have the crunch or the body of the iceburg but it is equally delicious.

Greek Style Lamb Burgers

- Serves: 4.
- Preparation time is 20 minutes.
- Inactive preparation time is 20 minutes.
- Cooking time is 1 hour.

Ingredients

1	pound ground lamb
1/2	fennel bulb, finely diced
2	shallots, finely diced
1 1/2	tablespoons olive oil, for sauteing
1	tablespoon margarine, for sauteing
	Sauce
1	cup mayonnaise
1 1/2	tablespoons garlic, minced
1	tablespoon anchovy paste
4	tomatoes, sliced
4	tablespoons margarine
4	hamburger buns

Instructions

Heat a water bath to 150°.

Saute the fennel and shallots in the olive oil and margarine until softened. Cool.

Combine the cooled fennel/shallot mixture with the lamb. Divide into one inch thick patties. Place each pattie into a separate bag and top with 1 tbls. margarine. Remove the air and seal. Place in the water bath. Cook for 1 hour.

Make the sauce by combining the mayonnaise, garlic, and anchovy paste.

Remove the burgers from the bags and place on buns. Top with sauce and sliced tomatoes. Enjoy.

Gyros with Tzatziki Sauce

- Serves: 6.
- Preparation time is 20 minutes.
- Inactive preparation time is 20 minutes.
- Cooking time is 30 minutes.

Ingredients

   2 pounds ground lamb
   3 tablespoons garlic powder
   1 tablespoon dried oregano
   1 tablespoon rosemary, ground
   2 teaspoons kosher salt
   1 medium onion, finely chopped
   Sauce
 16 ounces Plain nonfat Greek yogurt
   4 cloves garlic, minced
   1 medium cucumber, peeled
1/4 teaspoon kosher salt
   1 tablespoon red wine vinegar
   Condiments
   2 tomatoes, diced
   1 cucumber, sliced
   1 small onion, sliced
   6 pieces pita bread
   kalamata olives, sliced
   1 lettuce head, shredded
   1 tablespoon extra virgin olive oil, for searing

Instructions

Heat a water bath to 128 °.

To make the sauce, pour the yogurt into a cheesecloth lined strainer. Place the strainer over a large bowl so the liquid will drain. Let the yogurt drain for at least 2 1/2 hours or overnight in the refrigerator. Peel the cucumber and remove the seeds. Process in the food processor and remove to a tea towel. Squeeze out all of the moisture. Mix together the cucumber, yogurt, garlic, salt, olive oil and red wine vinegar. Refrigerate until ready to serve.

Mix the spices into the ground lamb. In a food processor, with a chopping blade, finely chop the onion. Remove the onion from the food processor and place in a tea towel. Squeeze out all of the moisture and return the onion to the food processor. Add the lamb to the food processor and process until the meat and onion mixture turn into a paste. Remove meat mixture from the processor and divide the meat into three different portions. Place each portion in an individual bag. With your hands, press down on the bag until the meat mixture is about 1/4 inch thick. Remove the air and seal. Place in the water bath. Cook for 30 minutes.

Remove meat from bags by cutting along sides of the bags and sliding the lamb onto an aluminum foil lined baking sheet. Top the meat with olive oil on both sides before searing. Sear the meat on both sides under the broiler or sear using a kitchen torch. Please note that the meat will continue to cook if you opt to sear it under the broiler. Cut meat into 1 inch wide stripes. Place strips of meat in pita bread and top with sauce and condiments.

Patti Melt

- Serves: 4.
- Preparation time is 20 minutes.
- Cooking time is 1 hour.

Ingredients

1 pound chuck roast, ground
1 large onion, thinly sliced
6 ounces mushrooms thinly sliced
8 slices rye bread
8 tablespoons margarine, plus 2 tablespoons
8 slices Provolone cheese

Instructions

Heat a water bath to 131°.

Divide the meat into four 1 inch thick equal size patties. The secret to a moist yummy burger is to place a Provolone cheese slice in the middle of each burger. Make sure to completely seal the cheese.

Place each pattie in an individual bag with 2 tbls. margarine. Remove the air and seal. Place in the water bath and cook for 1 hour.

Before serving, saute the onions and mushrooms in 2 tbls. of margarine. Cook until mixture is carmelized. Heat the broiler and spread the top of each piece of rye bread with margarine. Toast under the broiler. Remove from the broiler and top 4 of the toast with one slice of provolone cheese and melt under the broiler. Remove the burgers from their bags, and either brown in a hot skillet or use a cooking torch to brown. Place burger on the rye toast, and top with onion/mushrooms and remaining toast slices.

Sante Fe Pork Tacos

- Serves: 4.
- Preparation time is 10 minutes.
- Cooking time is 12 hours.

Ingredients

2 1/2 pounds pork shoulders, boston blade cut
1 tablespoon garlic powder, to sprinkle
1 tablespoon chili powder, to sprinkle
1 package taco seasoning
10 tablespoons margarine
4 brown rice tortillas
2 avocados, sliced
1 tablespoon lime juice
1 jar salsa
8 tablespoons sour cream

Instructions

Heat a water bath to 176°.

Season the pork shoulder with the garlic and chili powder on both sides. Cut the pork into 1 inch pieces. Place in a bag and add the taco seasoning making sure to coat the pieces. Top the meat with the margarine. Remove the air and seal. Place in the water bath. Cook for 12 hours.

Right before serving, prepare the avocados by slicing and mixing with the lime juice. Heat the tortillas and keep warm.

Remove the pork from the bag and shred. Top each tortilla with the salsa, avocados, and the sour cream.

Recipe Notes

To make garlic pulled pork, substitute seasonings for 3 Tbls. garlic paste and 2 Tbls. margarine.

Sirloin Burgers

- Serves: 3.
- Preparation time is 5 minutes.
- Cooking time is 1 hour.

Ingredients

    1 pound sirloin steak, ground
    1 tablespoon minced onion
    2 tablespoons Worcestershire sauce
    3 tablespoons margarine
    3 hamburger buns

Instructions

Heat a water bath to 130°.

Mix sirloin with minced onion and Worcestershire sauce. Form into 1 inch thick patties. Sear in a hot skillet to brown on both sides. Allow meat to cool. Place each pattie in an individual bag and top with margarine. Remove the air and seal. Place in the water bath and cook for one hour. Remove from bags and place on buns. Top with your favorite toppings and enjoy.

Sloppy Joes

- Serves: 4.
- Preparation time is 10 minutes.
- Inactive preparation time is 10 minutes.
- Cooking time is 3 hours.

Ingredients

      1 pound ground chuck
      1 small onion, chopped
    1/2 green pepper, finely diced
      2 tablespoons garlic powder
      2 tablespoons prepared yellow mustard
    3/4 cup organic ketchup
    1/4 cup barbecue sauce
      2 tablespoons olive oil, for sauteing
      8 slices thick bread
      8 tablespoons butter
         garlic powder, for sprinkling
      8 slices pepper jack cheese
      3 16 ounce ramekins

Instructions

Heat a water bath to 150°.

Saute the onions and green pepper in the olive oil until softened.
Remove from heat and cool.

In a large mixing bowl, add the meat, garlic powder, mustard, ketchup,
*barbecue sauce and cooled onion mixture. Mix well. Divide among
the ramekins. Place each ramekin in an individual bag and pulse to
seal. Place in water bath and cook for 3 hours.

Right before serving, toast the bread. Preheat the broiler. Butter each
piece of toast and sprinkle with garlic powder. Place on a baking
sheet and broil until lightly browned. Remove from broiler and turn
toast over to the other side. Top each piece of toast with a cheese
slice and broil until melted.

Remove Sloppy Joes from bags and spoon on top of cheese toast. Enjoy.

Recipe Notes

* Williamson Bros. Bar-B-Q Sauce was used in this recipe.

Meat

Brisket	77
Coney Dog Casserole	78
Cottage Pie	79
De-constructed Stuffed Cabbage	81
Egg Foo Young Frittata	83
Eggplant Lasagna	85
Inside Out Cordon Bleu over Cheese Fettuccine	87
Italian Pizza Custard	89
Italian Portabellos	91
Lamb Bourguignon	93
Lasagna Bolognese	94
London Broil	98
Pork Loins with Apple /Cranberry Stuffing	99
Reuben Lasagna	101
Scallion Encrusted Rack Of Lamb	103
Spaghetti Casserole	105
Spicy Chinese Short Ribs	107
Stuffed Center Cut Pork Chops	109
Stuffed Meat Loaf	111
Veal Chops in Marsala Sauce	113
Veal Scallopini with Prosciutto and Asparagus	115

Cooking Tables For Meats

TIMES ARE FOR THAWED NOT FROZEN MEATS

MINIMUM COOKING TIMES

	THICKNESS (INCHES)	MEDIUM RARE 126° - 135°	MEDIUM 136° - 140°	MEDIUM WELL 141° - 145°
MEAT	½	35 MIN.	35 MIN.	35 MIN.
MEAT	1	1 HOUR	1 HOUR	1 HOUR
MEAT	1 ½	1 ½ HOURS	1 ½ HOURS	1 ½ HOURS
MEAT	2	2 HOURS	2 HOURS	2 HOURS

	THICKNESS (INCHES)	MEDIUM 140°	MED. WELL 145°	WELL 176°
PORK	½	1 HOURS	2 HOUR	
PORK	1	2 HOURS	4 HOURS	
PORK	1 ½	3 HOURS	5 HOURS	
PORK	2	4 HOURS	6 HOURS	
PORK SHOULDER	2 - 3			12 HOURS
BEEF/ PORK RIBS	-			12 HOURS
BEEF/ PORK LAMB SHANKS	-			12 HOURS

Brisket

- Serves: 4.
- Preparation time is 5 minutes.
- Cooking time is 30 hours.

Ingredients

4 tablespoons margarine
1 packet onion soup mix
4 pounds beef brisket

Instructions

Heat a water bath to 135°.

Place the brisket in a bag. Place the margarine on top of the meat and sprinkle the onion soup mix on top. Remove the air and seal. Place in the water bath and cook for 30 hours. Remove the brisket from the bag and reserve the au jus in the bag. Slice and serve. Pour the au jus on top or reserve it for another time and freeze it in a bag.

Recipe Notes

Serve with sous vide cabbage and a great beer.

Coney Dog Casserole

- Serves: 3.
- Preparation time is 10 minutes.
- Cooking time is 30 minutes.

Ingredients

  1 medium onion, finely chopped
  2 tablespoons mustard
18 ounces baked beans, canned
  2 teaspoons molasses
  1 tablespoon mustard powder
  1 tablespoon ketchup
  1 tablespoon minced onion
  2 cups coney sauce (see recipe)
  1 cup extra sharp cheddar cheese, shredded
25 corn nacho chips
  6 hot dogs
  3 16 ounce ramekins

Instructions

Heat a water bath to 160°.

Mix the baked beans with the molasses, mustard powder, ketchup, and minced onion. Pour into the bottom of the 16 ounce ramekins.

Cut the hot dogs into bite size pieces and equally divide among the ramekins. Mix the prepared mustard with the finely chopped onions and spoon on top of the hot dogs. Equally portion out the coney sauce and top each ramekin. Place each ramekin in an individual bag and pulse to seal. Put in the bath and cook for a minimum of 30 minutes.

Make the nachos right before you are ready to serve. Preheat the broiler. Place the corn nacho chips on a baking sheet and top with shredded cheddar cheese. Place under the broiler and melt the cheese. Remove the ramekins from the bags and serve with the nachos.

Recipe Notes

Your favorite Beer or Root beer is highly recommended to accompany this dish.

Cottage Pie

- Serves: 5.
- Preparation time is 10 minutes.
- Inactive preparation time is 20 minutes.
- Cooking time is 3 1/2 hours.

Ingredients

    1 1/2 pounds lamb, ground
        8 ounces baby carrots
        1 medium onion, quartered
        2 tablespoons olive oil, for roasting
           cornstarch slurry
        1 cup beef stock
        1 tablespoon beef demi glace
       24 ounces prepared mashed potato
        1 cup frozen peas
        2 tablespoons horseradish
        5 16 ounce ramekins
        2 cups extra sharp cheddar cheese, shredded

Instructions

*Preheat an oven to 425°. Place carrots and quartered onions on a baking sheet lined with aluminum foil. Toss vegetables in olive oil to coat. Roast for 15 mins. and remove from oven. Turn carrots and onions to other side to evenly brown. Cook for another 15 mins. Remove from oven and cool. OR

Heat a water bath to 185°. Chop up the onion. Place vegetables in a bag with 2 tbls. margarine. Remove the air and seal. Place in water bath and keep submerged with plates. Cook for 2 hours. Remove from water bath. To remove the extra liquid from the bag, snip off a corner and allow the liquid to drain out. Cool.

Heat water bath to 150°.

To make the gravy, heat the beef stock in a saucepan. Add the demi glace. **Thicken the gravy with the cornstarch slurry. Remove from heat. Pour the gravy equally into the 16 ounce ramekins. Place the ramekins in the refrigerator to allow gravy to cool for approximately 20

the ramekins. Stir contents to coat with gravy. Place each ramekin into an individual bag and pulse to seal. The bag should be putting gentle pressure on top of the mixture. Do not be concerned if some of the gravy overflows from the ramekin. Place in the water bath and cook for 1 1/2 hours.

Put the prepared mashed potatoes into a large mixing bowl and mix in horseradish and half of the shredded cheddar cheese. Reserve the other half of the cheese for melting on top of the potatoes right before serving. Spoon potato mixture into a bag and pulse to seal. Place in the water bath to reheat along with the ramekins 1/2 hour before ready to serve.

Remove the ramekins from bags. Remove the potatoes from the water bath. Top each ramekin with the potato mixture. Sprinkle with reserved cheese. Melt with a cooking torch or under the broiler. Serve.

Recipe Notes

*Roasting the vegetables or cooking the vegetables using the sous vide method are merely a preference. Roasting imparts a sweeter flavor and sous videing the vegetables will maintain the flavor and nutrition.

**To make a cornstarch slurry, mix cold water with equal parts cornstarch. Slowly add the slurry to the gravy. If too much of the slurry is added the gravy will become to thick and have an unpleasant taste.

De-constructed Stuffed Cabbage

- Serves: 4.
- Preparation time is 15 minutes.
- Cooking time is 4 hours.

Ingredients

    1 medium cabbage, chopped
    1 pound ground beef
    3 tablespoons minced onion
 1/4 cup brown rice, cooked
 1/2 cup cream
    2 tablespoons garlic powder
    2 tablespoons garlic, minced
    3 tablespoons Worcestershire sauce
       salt, to taste
    6 tablespoons margarine
  30 ounces tomato soup
    4 16 ounce ramekins

Instructions

Heat a water bath to 183 °.

Remove the cores from the cabbage and chop. Place the cabbage into two bags and top each bag with 1 1/2 tbls. margarine. Remove the air and seal. Submerge in the water bath and weight down with plates. Cook for two hours. Remove the cabbage from bags and drain well. Let cool.

Lower the water bath to 140°.

Combine the meat with the minced onion, cooked brown rice, salt, garlic powder and minced garlic. In a separate bowl, combine the tomato soup, cream and the Worcestershire sauce. Stir half of the tomato soup mixture into the meat mixture. Reserve the other half of the sauce for finishing the dish. Divide the mixture between the ramekins. Top each with the cooked cabbage mixture. Place each ramekin in a separate bag and pulse to seal. Place in water bath for a minimum of 2 hours.

Heat the serving plates in a low temperature oven. Heat the reserved sauce mixture. To serve, remove the ramekins from the bags and turn each one out onto a heated plate. Top with the extra sauce and enjoy.

Egg Foo Young Frittata

- Serves: 4.
- Preparation time is 10 minutes.
- Inactive preparation time is 10 minutes.
- Cooking time is 2 hours.

Ingredients

1	pound pork shoulder, boston blade cut, cooked
2	large leeks, thinly sliced
3/4	pound mushrooms thinly sliced
4	tablespoons grapeseed oil, for sauteing
1/2	cup dry sherry
6.5	ounces bean sprouts
8	ounces water chestnut, sliced
6	eggs
2	tablespoons cream
4	16 ounce ramekins
24	ounces turkey gravy
2	bunches scallions, thinly sliced
1	small onion, thinly sliced

Instructions

Heat a water bath to 165°.

Saute the mushrooms in the grapeseed oil over high heat until browned. Lower the heat to medium and cook the onions and cleaned leeks until softened. Add the sherry and cook until it has evaporated. Remove from heat and cool.

Combine the bean sprouts, water chestnuts, and cooled mushroom/leek mixture. *Shred the pork and add it to the mixture. In a separate bowl, whisk the eggs and the cream. Stir the eggs into the pork mixture. Pour the mixture equally into the ramekins. Put each ramekin in an individual bag and pulse to seal. Place in the water bath and cook for 2 hours.

Prior to serving, warm the gravy in a sauce pan. Pour the gravy on top of the frittata and garnish with the scallions.

Recipe Notes

WARNING THIS RECIPE CONTAINS ALCOHOL.

*See the notes section under the recipe for Sante Fe tacos for the garlic pork recipe.

Eggplant Lasagna

- Serves: 4.
- Preparation time is 15 minutes.
- Inactive preparation time is 15 minutes.
- Cooking time is 1 hour and 25 minutes.

Ingredients

2	large eggplants, peeled & sliced lengthwise
1 1/2	tablespoons olive oil, for sauteing
1	tablespoon margarine, for sauteing
	cooking spray
1	medium onion, chopped
8	ounces mushrooms thinly sliced
1	tablespoon basil
1	tablespoon oregano
1 1/2	tablespoons garlic powder
4	ounces tomato paste
1/3	cup dry white wine
1/2	pound ground beef
2	Italian sausages
1/3	cup ricotta cheese
12	slices Provolone cheese
4	16 ounce ramekins

Instructions

Preheat oven to 400°.

Peel and slice the eggplant lengthwise into 1/4 inch thick slices. For this recipe, two slices per serving is needed. Place on a paper towel and salt the eggplants. This will cause the bitter juices to be released. Wait 20 minutes and flip the eggplants over and salt again. Place on new paper towels. Wait another 20 minutes. Dry the eggplants by patting dry. Line two baking sheets with aluminum foil and spray with the cooking spray. Place the eggplant on prepared baking sheets and spray the top of the eggplant with cooking spray. Place in the oven and cook for 15 minutes. Remove from oven and flip the eggplant to the other side. Cook for an additional 10 minutes. Watch the eggplant at this point because you do not want them to get too brown. Remove from oven and cool in the refrigerator.

While the eggplants are cooking, saute the mushrooms in 1 tbls. margarine over medium high heat. Lower heat to medium and add the olive oil and the onions. Add the basil and oregano and saute until the onions are translucent. Lower the heat to low. Move the mushrooms and onions towards the outer edge of the pan so that they will not continue to cook. Add the tomato paste to the pan and cook until it begins to brown. Add the white wine and deglaze the pan. Mix everything together and continue to cook on low until the sauce has tightened up and the alcohol has dissipated from the wine. Cool.

Preheat a water bath to 160°.

Mix the ground beef and sausage together. Add the cooled tomato sauce/vegetable mixture and combine well.

* Place one eggplant slice into the bottom of each ramekin. The eggplant slice may be larger then the bottom of the ramekin, if this is the case, allow the slice to go up the side of the ramekin. Place one slice of the Provolone cheese on top of the eggplant. Spoon the ricotta on top of the Provolone, followed by half of the meat mixture (equally dividing between the ramekins). Top the meat mixture with the remaining eggplant. Place one more slice of Provolone on top followed by the remaining meat mixture. Top off with the remaining Provolone slices. Place ramekins in an 11 inch wide bag (make sure you have plenty of length) and pulse to seal. Place in the water bath and cook for 1 hour.

Remove from bags and serve.

<u>Recipe Notes</u>

*You may also make this in a 9 x 5 loaf pan instead of individual ramekins.

Inside out Cordon Bleu over Cheese Fettucine

- Serves: 6.
- Preparation time is 15 minutes.
- Cooking time is 3 hours.

Ingredients

2 boneless skinless chicken breasts, cut into 1" cubes
6 slices black forest ham, 1/4 inch thick
6 slices extra sharp cheddar cheese
1/2 cup corn flakes, finely ground
4 tablespoons Parmesan cheese, grated
2 tablespoons dijon mustard
Sauce
4 ounces low fat cream cheese
1/4 cup dry sherry
6 ounces mushrooms thinly sliced
1/2 cup chicken stock
4 ounces fettuccine, cooked
1 tablespoon butter, for sauteing
2 cups swiss & gruyere cheese, shredded

Instructions

Heat a water bath to 150°.

Place one piece of cheddar cheese on each slice of ham. Evenly divide the chicken among the ham and place on top of the cheese. Fold one half of the ham over the chicken enclosing the mixture completely. Repeat the process. Place the ham in a bag. Remove the air and seal. Place in the water bath and cook for 3 hours.

*Make the sauce 15 minutes before serving. In a sauce pan, add the sherry and chicken stock. Bring to a boil and reduce to a simmer. Allow mixture to reduce by half. Remove from heat and allow to cool. Put the cream cheese and swiss/gruyere cheese in a blender. Add the cooled chicken stock and process until smooth. If mixture is too thick, add a little more chicken stock until desired consistency is reached. Pour mixture back into a sauce pan and keep mixture warm. Saute the mushrooms in butter until golden brown. Add the mushrooms to the warm cheese sauce.

Preheat a broiler on low.

Cook the pasta according to directions. Keep warm.

Combine the ground corn flakes with the parmesan cheese in a bowl. Remove the ham cordon bleu from bags and place on a large aluminum foil lined baking sheet. Spoon the dijon on one side of each ham cordon bleu. This will enable the breading to adhere. Spoon the corn flake/cheese mixture on top of each ham slice. **Place under the broiler until lightly browned.   Plate the pasta and top with the mushroom sauce. Place the ham cordon bleu on top of the fettuccine. Serve.

Recipe Notes

WARNING THIS RECIPE CONTAINS ALCOHOL

* Make the sauce ahead of time and refrigerate it. Place it in the water bath to reheat.

** A kitchen torch may be used to melt/brown the cheese/corn flake topping.

Italian Pizza Custard

- Serves: 4.
- Preparation time is 15 minutes.
- Cooking time is 2 1/2 hours.

Ingredients

     8 ounces low fat cream cheese
   1/2 cup ricotta cheese
     2 tablespoons tomato paste
     3 tablespoons garlic paste
     4 eggs
   1/2 cup mixed black olives, chopped
   1/2 cup sweet pepper rings
     6 ounces jar of sliced mushrooms, drained
    20 slices pepperoni
     1 small onion, chopped
     1 tablespoon basil
     1 tablespoon oregano
     2 cups mixed salad greens
     2 tablespoons Italian salad dessing
     4 4" dia. spring form pans

Instructions

Heat a water bath to 160°.

Using an electric beater, cream together the cream cheese and ricotta. Add the tomato paste and eggs. When the ingredients have been thoroughly combined, mix in by hand the sweet pepper rings, mushrooms, and olives. In the bottom of the spring form pans, layer 5 slices of pepperoni making sure to completely cover the bottom of the pans. Pour in the cream cheese mixture, evenly dividing among the pans. Top with the other 5 slices of pepperoni. Seal in an individual bag by pulsing until the bag begins to put pressure on top of the pepperoni. Place in the water bath and cook for 2 1/2 hours.

Remove the spring form pans from the bags and allow them to cool to room temperature.

Ten minutes before serving, saute the onions with the basil and oregano in a little olive oil. Place the mixed greens on serving plates and dress with the Italian dressing. Turn the spring form pans upside down on the mixed greens and remove the sides and the bottom of the pans. Top with the onion/herb mixture.

Italian Portabellos

- Serves: 4.
- Preparation time is 15 minutes.
- Inactive preparation time is 15 minutes.
- Cooking time is 2 hours.

Ingredients

- 10 pepperoni, sliced
- 3 large portabello mushrooms
- 1 small onion, finely chopped
- 1 teaspoon basil
- 1 teaspoon oregano
- 1 tablespoon garlic powder
- 1 Italian sausage, casings removed
- 1/2 cup ricotta cheese
- 1/2 cup Parmesan cheese, grated
- 2 tablespoons tomato paste
- 1 package fresh baby spinach
- 1 tablespoon olive oil, for sauteing
- 1 grapeseed oil, for searing

Instructions

Heat a water bath to 161°.

Saute the onions and spices in the olive oil until soft. Cool. Mix together the ricotta, sausage, pepperoni, tomato paste, onion mixture, and Parmesan.

Clean the mushrooms and remove the stems. Put a little grapeseed oil on the mushroom caps. Using a kitchen torch, brown and sear the mushroom caps (flesh side up not the underside) or quickly sear in a hot skillet. Stuff each mushroom with the ricotta mixture. Put each mushroom in an individual bag. Pulse to seal. Place in a water bath and cook for 2 hours.

Heat plates in an oven (185°) and top with the spinach. The heat will wilt the spinach. This should be done about 15 minutes prior to serving. Remove the mushrooms and place on top of the spinach. Enjoy.

Recipe Notes

This is a great substitute for pizza for your guests who have gluten/wheat allergies.

Lamb Bourguignon

- Serves: 4.
- Preparation time is 20 minutes.
- Inactive preparation time is 20 minutes.
- Cooking time is 12 hours.

Ingredients

  4 lamb shanks
  2 tablespoons garlic powder
  2 tablespoons rosemary
  2 tablespoons thyme
  2 tablespoons grapeseed oil
16 ounces pappardelle noodles
  8 tablespoons butter
  2 cups Bourguignon sauce, see recipe

Instructions

Heat a water bath to 176°.

Season the shanks with the garlic powder, rosemary and thyme. Sear the shanks on all sides in a hot skillet with the grapeseed oil. Remove from heat. Allow to cool in the refreigerator. Place shanks in a bag and pulse to seal. Cook for 12 hours.

Remove the shanks from the water bath. Clip off a corner of the bag and allow the liquid to drain out. Reserve the liquid or discard. Remove shanks from bag and shred the meat. * Place the meat in the prepared Bourguignon sauce (see recipe). Prepare the noodles and toss with 2 tbls. butter per serving. Top the noodles with the lamb in Bourguignon sauce. Serve.

Recipe Notes

*Another option is to prepare the sauce and the lamb ahead of time and combine. Place in a loaf pan and put in a bag and pulse to seal. Place in a 176° water bath to reheat for approximately 30 minutes.

Lasagna Bolognese

- Serves: 4.
- Preparation time is 20 minutes.
- Inactive preparation time is 20 minutes.

<u>Ingredients</u>

6	ounces sliced mushrooms
1	tablespoon butter
1/4	cup Parmesan cheese, grated, for garnish
8	lasagne noodles, cooked
1	9"x5"glass loaf pan

<u>Bolognese Sauce</u>

2	tablespoons grapeseed oil
1 1/2	pounds pork shanks, on the bone
1 1/2	pounds beef shanks, on the bone
1/2	pound pancetta, diced
3/4	cup Spanish onion, finely chopped
1/4	cup carrot, finely chopped
1/4	cup celery, finely chopped
1	teaspoon garlic powder
1/2	cup dry red wine
1 1/2	cups beef stock
7 1/2	ounces can diced tomatoes, and its juices
1	teaspoon dried thyme
1	tablespoon dried rosemary

<u>Tomato Sauce</u>

1 1/2	tablespoons olive oil
1	medium onion, finely chopped
2	cloves garlic, finely minced
1	teaspoon crushed red chili flakes
14 1/2	ounces crushed tomatoes, and its juices
8	ounces tomato sauce
1 1/2	tablespoons dried basil

<u>Bechamel Sauce</u>

4	ounces low fat cream cheese
8	ounces heavy cream
8	ounces Fontina cheese
1/4	cup Parmesan cheese
1/4	cup beef stock

<u>Ricotta Mixture</u>
   1 cup ricotta cheese
1/2 cup Parmesan cheese, grated
1/3 cup fresh basil, chiffonade

<u>Instructions</u>

Heat a water bath to 176°.

Bolognese Sauce
Heat the grapeseed oil in a large skillet over high heat. Add the shanks to the hot oil in batches. Brown on all sides. Remove to a plate and refrigerate until cooled and ready to assemble. Pour off fat except for 1 tbls. Lower the heat to medium and add 1/3 of the pancetta and cook until browned. Remove with a slotted spoon to a plate lined with paper towels. Refrigerate.

Remove all of the fat from the skillet except for 1 tbls. Over medium heat, add the onion, carrots, celery and garlic powder and cook until soft and lightly golden brown. Add the thyme and rosemary. Cook for another minute. Add the red wine and scrape the bottom of the pan. Cook until the wine is completely reduced. Add the beef broth and the diced tomatoes. Cook for 5 minutes. Remove from heat. Refrigerate until cooled.

Cut off the excess fat from the meat. * Place the browned meat and the 1/3 cooked pancetta into the loaf pan. Pour the cooled vegetable sauce over the meat. Place the loaf pan in a bag and pulse to seal. Place in the water bath and cook for 48 hours.

Remove the loaf pan from water bath. Cut open the bag and carefully remove the loaf pan. Pour any sauce which may have accumulated in the bags back into the loaf pan. Remove the meat from the broth and shred. Discard the fat and the bones. Pour the sauce through a sieve and into a bowl. Discard vegetable mixture. The reserved sauce will be added to the Tomato Sauce later. Put the meat and the reserved sauce (if you will be making the tomato sauce, it is not necessary to refrigerate the reserved sauce) into the refrigerator to cool.

Heat a skillet over high heat. Add the butter to the pan and melt. Add the sliced mushrooms and cook until golden brown. Remove from pan to a plate and refrigerate. Lower the heat to medium and add the remaining pancetta to the pan. Cook until golden brown and remove with a slotted spoon to a plate lined with paper towel. Refrigerate.

Tomato Sauce
Add olive oil to a medium size saucepan. Over medium heat, saute the onions and garlic. Add the red chili flakes. Add the crushed tomatoes, tomato sauce and the basil. Add the reserved sauce from the meat to the sauce. Simmer over medium heat for 1/2 an hour. Pour into a bowl and refrigerate until cool.

Bechamel Sauce
In a food processor, process the cream cheese, Fontina cheese, and Parmesan cheese. Slowly add the cream while the machine is running. Stop and scrape down the sides of the bowl. Process again and add the beef stock. Refrigerate the sauce until ready to assemble.

Ricotta Cheese Mixture
Combine the ricotta, Parmesan and half of the chiffonaded basil. Refrigerate until ready to assemble.

Prepare the pasta and allow to cool.

Heat a water bath to 150°.

To assemble the Lasagna, place a little Bechamel Sauce in the bottom of a glass loaf pan. Add two noodles (overlapping) to the bottom. Spoon the Ricotta mixture on top. Add two more lasgana noodles (overlapping). Spoon 1/2 of the meat mixture (Bolognese) on top of the pasta. Sprinkle half of the mushrooms and pancetta over the meat. Top the meat (Bolognese) with just enough Tomato Sauce to cover the meat. Top the Tomato Sauce with more Bechamel Sauce making sure to cover the meat completely. Sprinkle a little Parmesan cheese over sauce. Add another layer of meat (Bolgenese) followed by the mushrooms and pancetta. Spoon enough Tomato Sauce over the meat to cover (there will be some Tomato Sauce and pasta leftover which will be reserved for finishing). Top with the Bechamel Sauce again. Cover the tomato/meat sauce completely. Add the reserved chiffonade of basil on top. Place the loaf pan carefully into a bag. Pulse to seal and place in the water bath. Cook for 1 hour.

The remaining pasta is placed flat into a bag and pulse to seal. Place in the water bath alongside the lasagna to keep warm.

Prior to serving, heat the remaining reserved Tomato Sauce. Remove the lasagna from the bag and divide into serving sizes. Plate. Remove the pasta from the bag by cutting along the sides of the bag. Lift out the pasta. Cut each noodle in half and place on top of each serving of lasagna. Spoon the hot Tomato Sauce on top and garnish with Parmesan.

Recipe Notes

WARNING THIS RECIPE CONTAINS ALCOHOL

*It may be necessary to divide the meat between two loaf pans. If this is the case, equally divide the sauce among the two loaf pans.

Cooking time for meats are for 48 hours.

Cooking time for the lasagna is 1 hour.

Tip: prepare the sauces ahead of time and assemble the lasagna.

London Broil

- Serves: 6.
- Preparation time is 10 minutes.
- Cooking time is 12 hours.

Ingredients

4 pounds london broil
2 tablespoons garlic powder
2 tablespoons grapeseed oil
salt, to taste
pepper, to taste
6 tablespoons margarine

Instructions

Heat a water bath to 134°.

Heat a skillet on high. *Add the grapeseed oil and place the seasoned meat in skillet to brown. This should only take two minutes each side. Remove the meat and allow to cool in the refrigerator.

Place the margarine and the meat in a large bag. Remove the air and seal. Place in water bath for 12 hours. Remove from bath and let rest five minutes covered with aluminum foil. Slice and serve on warmed plates.

Recipe Notes

*The meat should not be more than 2 inches in thickness. Ask your butcher to cut the meat into two separate servings. It is not recommended to cook below 134° for longer then four hours. This temperature is for medium rare/ medium. If a more rare temperature is desired, use a jacquard (tool which punches small holes in meat) on the meat and marinate in an acid base marinade for 24 hours. This will make the meat more tender. Cook at a lower temperature (never below 128°) for the minimum of two hours and the maximum of 4 hours.

Pork Loins with Apple/Cranberry Stuffing

- Serves: 4.
- Preparation time is 20 minutes.
- Inactive preparation time is 20 minutes.
- Cooking time is 4 hours.

Ingredients

    4 1 inch thick pork loins, butterflied
    1 tablespoon poultry seasoning
 1/2 cup celery, finely diced
 1/2 cup scallions, thinly sliced
 1/2 cup dried orange cranberries
    3 cups bread, dried & cubed
    1 cup beef stock
    1 granny smith apple, finely diced
       Sauce
    4 large oranges, juiced
    2 teaspoons fresh ginger, grated
    6 tablespoons soy sauce
    4 tablespoons honey
    2 tablespoons dijon mustard
    5 tablespoons margarine

Instructions

Heat a water bath to 140°.

Heat 1 tbls. margarine in a skillet and saute the celery, scallions, and apples. Add 1 tbls. poultry seasoning. Cook until ingredients have softened.

Place the dried bread cubes in a mixing bowl. Add the vegetable mixture to the bread. Add the orange cranberries. Slowly add the beef stock until the bread is softened. You may need to add a little more stock or less. Lightly sprinkle a little more poultry seasoning on top and mix thoroughly. Pour mixture into a bag and pulse to seal. Place in the water bath to cook along with the pork loins.

Place each pork loin into individual bags. Top each loin with 1 tbls. margarine. Remove the air and seal. Cook for 4 hours.

Make the sauce 30 minutes prior to serving. Add the last six ingredients to a sauce pan and bring to a boil. Reduce heat and simmer on low, covered, for about 10 mins. Keep warm.

Remove pork loins and the stuffing from bags. Stuff each loin with the stuffing and place on warmed plates. Top with sauce. Serve.

Reuben Lasagna

- Serves: 2.
- Preparation time is 10 minutes.
- Cooking time is 2 hours and 45 minutes.

<u>Ingredients</u>

1	large yukon gold potato, peeled & thinly sliced
2	tablespoons butter
2	tablespoons thousand island salad dressing
2	cups Swiss cheese, shredded
1/4	cup sauerkraut, canned, drained
2	slices rye bread, 1/2 inch cubes
1 1/2	tablespoons butter
1/3	package low fat cream cheese
1/2	pound corned beef, 1/2 inch cubes
2	16 ounce ramekins

<u>Instructions</u>

Heat water bath to 185 °.

Peel the potato and slice thin in a food processor. Place slices in a bag with the 2 tbls. butter and seal removing all of the air. Place in the water bath and weight down with plates. Cook for 2 hours. Remove from water bath and take potatoes out of the bag. Let potatoes cool.

Lower the water bath to 140°.

Put the cream cheese, thousand island dressing, and one cup of the swiss cheese in a blender and process until smooth. The remaining cup of cheese will be reserved for later which will be melted on top of the lasagna. Place 1/2 of the cheese mixture (divided equally) in each ramekin and top with 1/2 of the cooled potatoes. Divide the meat mixture into four equal portions. Place half of one portion of the meat on top of the potatoes followed by the sauerkraut (equally divided) into each ramekin. Equally divide and place the remaining 1/2 of the potatoes on top of the sauerkraut followed by the remaining meat. Press down on the mixture to compact. Top with the remaining cheese/ thousand island mixture. Place in individual bags. Pulse machine until the bag begins to put pressure on top of the food. Place in the water bath and cook for 45 mins.

Preheat broiler on low. About 5 minutes prior to serving, prepare the rye bread. In an oven safe skillet, over medium heat, heat the 1 1/2 tbls. butter. Add the rye bread cubes and coat well in melted butter. Cook until the butter has been completely absorbed by the rye bread cubes. Remove the skillet from the stove and place the skillet in the oven on the lowest rack. Remove the ramekins from the water bath and the bags. Top the ramekins with the reserved Swiss cheese. Place under the broiler and melt until lightly browned and bubbly. Top with the rye bread croutons. Serve.

Scallion Encrusted Rack of Lamb

- Serves: 4.
- Preparation time is 15 minutes.
- Cooking time is 4 hours.

<u>Ingredients</u>

```
  2  racks of lamb
  4  tablespoons mayonnaise
  4  tablespoons dijon mustard
  2  bunches scallions, sliced
1/2  cup bread crumbs
1/4  teaspoon red pepper flakes
  4  tablespoons margarine
  2  tablespoons garlic powder
1/2  cup grapeseed oil, for searing
  2  tablespoons olive oil, for sauteing
  2  tablespoons garlic, minced
```

<u>Instructions</u>

Heat a water bath to 130°.

Pat the lamb racks dry with paper towels.   Heat a skillet on high. When pan is very hot, add the grapeseed oil and the lamb racks. Sear just until browned on all sides. Let cool. Refrigerate until ready to cook.

Season the cooled lamb with the garlic powder. Place the racks in an individual bag and top with the margarine. Remove the air and seal. Place in the water bath. Cook for 4 hours.

Just before the lamb is ready to be served, heat the olive oil in a skillet over medium heat. Add the sliced scallions and the minced garlic and cook until softened. Add the bread crumbs and the red pepper flakes. Stir to combine. Cook for approximately 2 minutes until bread crumbs are cooked through. Remove from heat.

Mix together the mayonnaise and dijon.

Remove the lamb from the bag. Spread the mayo/dijon mixture on top. Top with the bread crumb mixture. * Using a kitchen torch, brown the mayo/bread crumb mixture or place under a preheated broiler and brown. Serve.

<u>Recipe Notes</u>

*If you brown the lamb under the broiler it will cook the meat more. If you want the meat to be medium rare, and you will be broiling the topping, cook the lamb at a lower water bath temperature of 128°.

Cooking times are for 2 inch thick lamb. It is not recommended that food cooked at 130° or lower be cooked for more then 4 hours.

Spaghetti Casserole

- Serves: 4.
- Preparation time is 15 minutes.
- Inactive preparation time is 15 minutes.
- Cooking time is 1 1/2 hours.

<u>Ingredients</u>

    2 pounds frozen spinach, defrosted
1/2 pound spaghetti, cooked
 16 ounces marinara sauce
   1 cup Parmesan cheese, grated
 12 slices Provolone cheese
   2 Italian sausages
   8 eggs
   4 tablespoons cream
   2 tablespoons garlic paste
   4 16 ounce oval ramekins

<u>Instructions</u>

Heat a water bath to 165°.

Cook the pasta according to package directions. Drain and cool. Let the pasta dry. Defrost the spinach and squeeze all of the water out of it.

Whisk together the eggs, cream, garlic paste, and Parmesan cheese. In another bowl, stir the marinara sauce into the dry cooked spaghetti. Reserve enough sauce to top each ramekin before serving. Heat the sauce in a sauce pan before serving. Keep warm.

Pour half of the egg mixture equally among the oval ramekins. Equally divide the spaghetti mixture and place on top of the eggs. Top with the spinach and crumble the sausage. Pour the remaining egg mixture on top. Place two pieces of provolone on top of the egg mixture covering the eggs. * Place each ramekin in an individual bag and pulse to seal. Place in the water bath and cook for 1 1/2 hours.

Remove the ramekins from the bags and place on top of a plate. Portion out the warmed marinara sauce and place on top of the casserole. Serve.

Recipe Notes

*The egg mixture may overflow the ramekin a little.

 Make this a vegetarian dish by eliminating the sausage.

Spicy Chinese Short Ribs

- Serves: 4.
- Preparation time is 10 minutes.
- Inactive preparation time is 10 minutes.
- Cooking time is 12 hours.

Ingredients

    2 tablespoons grapeseed oil, for searing
    8 large short ribs
      Sauce
  12 tablespoons hoisin sauce
    4 tablespoons ketchup
    4 tablespoons dry sherry
    4 tablespoons white wine vinegar
    4 tablespoons honey
    4 teaspoons lemon juice
    4 teaspoons fresh ginger, grated
    1 teaspoon chinese five spice
  1/4 teaspoon red pepper flakes
    1 bunch scallions, finely chopped

Instructions

Heat a water bath to 176°.

Heat a skillet over high heat. Add the grapeseed oil to the pan. The oil should be rippling. In batches, sear the ribs on all sides until brown. Do not crowd the pan or the ribs will have difficulty browning. Place on a plate and allow to cool. Refrigerate until ready to cook.

Make the sauce by adding the remaining ingredients (except the scallions) to a sauce pan. Bring sauce to a boil and reduce to a simmer. Simmer for 10 minutes. Remove sauce pan from heat and allow to cool in the refrigerator.

Divide and place the cooled short ribs into two separate bags. Add and divide half of the sauce between the two bags. The other half of the sauce will be heated and placed on top of the ribs for serving. Coat the ribs well with the sauce. Pulse to seal. Place in the water bath. Cook for a minimum of 12 hours.

Ten minutes prior to serving, reheat the reserved sauce. Remove short ribs from bag. Plate. Pour sauce on top of the ribs and garnish with chopped scallions.

Stuffed Center Cut Porkchops

- Serves: 4.
- Preparation time is 15 minutes.
- Cooking time is 8 hours.

Ingredients

<pre>
4   pork chops, center cut, 4 ounces each, 1 1/2" thick
3   tablespoons grapeseed oil, for searing
2   tablespoons garlic powder
3   tablespoons sun-dried tomatoes in oil, julienned
1   package frozen spinach, defrosted
3   ounces low fat cream cheese
2   ounces goat cheese with herbs
1   small onion, chopped
6   tablespoons margarine
     Sauce
1/2 cup chicken stock
1   tablespoon lemon zest
1   tablespoon lemon juice
2   tablespoons dijon mustard
</pre>

Instructions

*Heat a water bath to 140°.

Squeeze the moisture out of the defrosted spinach. Saute the onions in 2 tbls. margarine and let cool. Drain the sun-dried tomatoes and julienne.

In a hot skillet, add the grapeseed oil. Sear the chops on both sides until browned. You may use a kitchen torch to sear instead. Remove from skillet and cool.

Pat dry the chops and carefully butterfly open or ask your butcher to do it for you. Combine the spinach, onions, sun-dried tomatoes, cream cheese, and goat cheese. Place the mixture onto one side of each chop. Fold the other side of the butterflied chop over the mixture. Sprinkle each chop with the garlic powder on both sides. Place each chop in an individual bag and top with 1 tbls. each margarine. Remove the air and seal. Place in water bath. Cook for 8 hours.

To make the sauce, heat the chicken stock in a sauce pan and add the lemon juice, zest and dijon. Bring to a boil and reduce to a simmer. Pour over cooked chops and enjoy.

Recipe Notes

*This temperature is for a medium chop. Raise or lower the temperature of the water bath according to desired doneness.

Stuffed Meat Loaf

- Serves: 4.
- Preparation time is 15 minutes.
- Cooking time is 4 hours.

<u>Ingredients</u>

        1 pound ground beef
        1 pound ground pork
        1 tablespoon olive oil
        1 small onion, chopped
        8 ounces baby carrots, shredded
        1 package onion soup mix
        1 jar roasted red peppers, drained
        8 slices pepper jack cheese
        4 tablespoons margarine
           <u>Sauce</u>
    2 1/2 cups tomatoes, diced
        1 small onion, sliced
        1 teaspoon cinnamon
      1/4 cup brown sugar
        1 teaspoon red wine vinegar
        1 teaspoon salt
        4 4" mini loaf pans

<u>Instructions</u>

For the sauce, combine the tomatoes, onion, cinnamon, brown sugar, red wine vinegar and salt. Simmer on low heat for 2 hours. Puree the sauce and keep warm until ready to serve.

Heat a water bath to 140°

Over medium heat, add the olive oil and saute the onions and carrots until softened. Let cool. Drain the red peppers and pat dry. Slice the red peppers into strips.

Combine the beef, pork, and soup mix. Add the cooled carrots/onions to the meat and mix until well combined. Divide the mixture in half and equally portion each half. Place in each mini loaf pan, half of the portioned meat mixture. Top the meat mixture with one slice pepper jack cheese followed by the red pepper strips. Place another pepper jack slice on top of the red pepper strips. Put the other half of the meat mixture on top of the cheese pressing firmly. Repeat this process with the other mini loaf pans. Place each loaf pan in an individual bag and top with one tbls. margarine. Pulse to seal. The bag should be pressing down firmly on top of the meat. Cook for 4 hours minimum.

Heat plates in an oven. Remove the meat loaf from the bags and turn out onto the warmed plates. Top with sauce and serve.

Veal Chops in Marsala Sauce

- Serves: 4.
- Preparation time is 20 minutes.
- Inactive preparation time is 20 minutes.
- Cooking time is 4 hours.

Ingredients

        1   tablespoon butter
      1/4   cup canola oil
        4   veal chops, 2"thickness or less
        2   tablespoons garlic paste
        6   ounces mushrooms thinly sliced
        1   pepper, to taste
        1   salt, to taste
        6   green onions, thinly sliced
    1 1/2   cups beef broth
      1/4   cup Marsala Wine
        2   tablespoons cornstarch slurry

Instructions

Heat a water bath to 140°.

In a very hot skillet add the oil. Sear the veal chops on both sides until browned. Remove the chops from the skillet and let the chops cool. Pour off all but 2 tbls. of the hot oil.

On medium high heat, add the butter to the remaining oil in the skillet. Add the mushrooms to the skillet. When the mushrooms have browned and reduced in size, add the green onions to the skillet. Cook the green onions until they have softened (about 2 mins.). Add the garlic paste and stir into mushroom/ onion mixture. Add the Marsala wine and cook for 2 mins. Add the beef broth and cook until warmed. Stir in half of the *cornstarch slurry. Keep stirring until the broth begins to thicken. If the consistency is not thick enough, add more of the cornstarch slurry into the sauce. A little goes a long ways so be cautious in adding more. If the sauce becomes too thick add more beef broth. Remove the sauce from the heat and cool. **When the sauce has cooled pour into two 11 inch wide bags, dividing the sauce equally. Seal the bags but do not remove the air. Place the bags into the freezer. Allow the sauce to set up for about 20 mins.

After the sauce has set up, open the bags and put two chops in each bag. Using the pulse on the machine, remove the air from the bags and seal. Place the bags into the water bath and cook for 4 hrs. About a 1/2 hour prior to plating the chops, warm the plates in the oven. Remove the chops from bags and plate. Pour the sauce over the top of the chops and serve.

Recipe Notes

WARNING THIS RECIPE CONTAINS ALCOHOL.

* a cornstarch slurry is equal parts of cornstarch and cold water mixed together until dissolved.

** Allow enough length on the bags to cut open and put the chops inside as well as resealing for cooking.

Veal Scallopine with Prosciutto and Asparagus

- Serves: 2.
- Preparation time is 5 minutes.
- Cooking time is 3 hours.

Ingredients

  4 large veal cutlets, 1/4 inch thick
  4 slices prosciutto
  4 slices Provolone cheese
20 asparagus
  6 tablespoons margarine

Instructions

Heat a water bath to 140°.

Prepare the asparagus (see recipe).

Place one piece of prosciutto on one piece of veal. Top with one slice of provolone and ten asparagus followed by another slice of provolone. * Place another veal cutlet on top trying to enclose the filling. Repeat with the other cutlets. Place the cutlets in an individual bag topped with 3 tbls. margarine. Remove the air and seal. Place in the water bath. Cook for three hours.

Heat plates in a warm oven. Remove cutlets from bags and plate. Pour butter sauce from bags on top and serve.

Recipe Notes

*When purchasing the veal cutlets try to match up the size of the cutlets. This will enable the filling to be enclosed.

Poultry

Asian Duck Breasts 118
Black Forest Chicken 120
Chicken Margarita 122
Chicken Parmesan 123
Chicken Prosciutto Pie 125
Creamy Chicken and Wild Mushroom Casserole 127
De-constructed Chicken Pot Pie 129
Italian Chicken Zucchini Bundles 131
Lemon Chicken 133
Orange Garlic Five Spice Injected Chicken 135
Pheasant with Orange Madeira Sauce 136
Tandoori Chicken with Raita Sauce 137
Yummy Turkey Breast 139

Cooking Tables For Poultry

TIMES ARE FOR THAWED NOT FROZEN

PLEASE ADD 30 MINUTES TO COOKING TIME FOR BONE IN

POULTRY	THICKNESS (INCHES)	TEMPERATURE	COOKING TIMES (MINIMUM TIME)
CHICKEN	½	150°	30 MINUTES
CHICKEN	1	150°	40 MINUTES
CHICKEN	1 ½	150°	1 ½ HOURS
CHICKEN	2	150°	2 HOURS
DUCK	1	134°	2 HOURS AND 25 MINUTES
DUCK CONFIT	3	176°	8 HOURS*
PHEASANT (2 ½ LBS)	-	140°	5 HOURS

* ADDITIONAL 30 MINUTES NOT REQUIRED

Asian Duck Breasts

- Serves: 6.
- Preparation time is 10 minutes.
- Cooking time is 3 hours.

Ingredients

     6 duck breasts, 1 inch thick
        garlic powder, to sprinkle
        chinese five spice, to sprinkle
        Sauce
     2 cups pitted plums, chopped
 1/2 cup honey
     4 garlic cloves, minced
     4 tablespoons white wine vinegar
     2 tablespoons hoisin sauce
     1 teaspoon red pepper flakes
 1/2 cup scallions, sliced for garnish
        cracklings, for garnish
     6 tablespoons margarine
        cooking spray

Instructions

Heat a water bath to 134°.

Carefully remove the skin from the duck breasts and reserve. The skin/fat will be cooked later and served as a garnish. Lightly sprinkle one side of each breast with the garlic powder and chinese five spice. Place each breast in an individual bag and top with 1 tbls. margarine. Remove the air and seal. Place in the water bath. Cook for three hours.

To make the sauce, combine the plums, honey, garlic cloves, white wine vinegar, hoisin sauce and red pepper flakes in a saucepan. Simmer over low heat until the plums have completely softened. Puree in a blender or use a hand blender. Keep warm.

To make the cracklings, preheat an oven to 400°. Place reserved skins on a baking sheet lined with aluminum foil and sprayed with cooking spray. Top the skins with another piece of aluminum foil which has been lightly sprayed with cooking spray. Weight down with an oven proof skillet. Cook for approximately 1/2 hour or until skins have completely browned. Remove from the oven and allow to cool.

Remove breasts from bags and plate. Top with sauce and garnish with sliced scallions and crumbled skin (cracklings).

Black Forest Chicken Stew

- Serves: 8.
- Preparation time is 20 minutes.
- Inactive preparation time is 20 minutes.
- Cooking time is 4 hours.

Ingredients

    1 pound kielbasa sausage, cut into 1/2" cubes
    2 chicken breasts, boneless & skinless, 1/2 inch cubes
   16 small cipollini onions
1 1/2 pounds mixed mushrooms, thinly sliced
    4 medium yukon gold potatoes, 1/2 inch cubes
    6 tablespoons margarine
  1/2 quart sauerkraut, canned
    4 tablespoons caraway seeds
      Sauce
    4 tablespoons spicy brown mustard
    8 ounces low fat cream cheese
    1 cup chicken stock
    4 16 ounce ramekins

Instructions

Heat a water bath to 185°.

Bring four cups of water to a boil in a small sauce pan. Drop the onions in the water and cook for 3 minutes. Remove the onions from the water and place in an ice bath for 2 minutes. Remove the onions from the ice bath and peel off the skins.

Place the cleaned and cubed potatoes with the peeled onions and 3 Tbls. margarine in a bag. *Remove the air and seal. Place in the water bath and cook for 2 hours.

Melt the remaining 3 tbls. margarine over high heat. Add the mushrooms and cook until they have browned and reduced in size. Remove from heat and cool.

Prepare the sauce in a blender by adding the chicken stock, mustard, and cream cheese. Process until smooth. The sauce will be thick.

Divide the mushrooms, chicken and kielbasa between the 16 ounce ramekins. Add enough sauce to mix through. Reserve the remaining sauce by placing in a small ramekin and placing in a bag. Pulse to seal. You will place the sauce ramekin in the water bath with the others to keep warm. Place each ramekin in an individual bag and pulse to seal. Keep in the refrigerator until ready to cook.

*After the vegetables have cooked, lower the water bath to 151°. Keep the vegetables in the bath to keep warm. When the water bath has cooled add the meat ramekins and the sauce ramekin to the bath and cook for 2 hours.

Preheat a regular oven to 175° thirty minutes before the meal is ready. Divide the sauerkraut and place on the serving plates. Keep the plates warm in the oven until ready to serve. Toast the caraway seeds in a small skillet on top of the stove. Sprinkle equally on top of the sauerkraut. Remove potatoes/onions from bag and evenly divide among plates on top of sauerkraut. Remove the ramekins from bags and place contents equally divided on top of the sauerkraut/ potato mixture. Remove the sauce ramekin from the bag and portion evenly on top of the meat mixture. Serve and enjoy.

Recipe Notes

*If you have two water baths you will be able to cook the meal simultaneously.

Chicken Margarita

- Serves: 4.
- Preparation time is 10 minutes.
- Cooking time is 3 hours.

Ingredients

    4 boneless skinless chicken breasts
    4 slices prosciutto
    6 medium tomatoes, sliced
    4 tablespoons margarine
    8 slices Provolone cheese, 4" diameter
    1 head garlic, thinly sliced
1/2 cup dry white wine
    4 tablespoons pesto sauce
    4 tablespoons margarine, for sauce
    1 cup fresh basil, chiffonade

Instructions

Heat a water bath to 150°.

Place a slice of prosciutto on top of each breast. Spread one tbls. of pesto on top of each breast followed by two slices of the provolone. Equally divide the tomatoes and place on top of the cheese. Place each breast in an individual bag. Remove the air and seal. Place in the water bath and cook for 3 hours.

To make the wine sauce, heat the 1 tbls. margarine over low heat. Add the sliced garlic and cook until lightly browned. Add the white wine and reduce by half. Add the remaining margarine to the pan. Remove the chicken from the bags and plate. Pour the sauce over the chicken and garnish with the fresh basil.

Recipe Notes

WARNING THIS RECIPE CONTAINS ALCOHOL.

The cooking time is for 1 to 1 1/2 inch thick breasts.

Classico pesto sauce was used in this recipe.

Chicken Parmesan

- Serves: 4.
- Preparation time is 20 minutes.
- Inactive preparation time is 20 minutes.
- Cooking time is 3 hours.

Ingredients

  4 boneless skinless chicken breasts
 28 ounces chunky tomato sauce
  4 tablespoons garlic paste
 14 ounces fettuccine, cooked
 18 slices Provolone cheese, 4" diameter
  4 16 ounce ramekins
  1 tablespoon garlic powder, for sprinkling
  4 cups bread crumbs
  2 tablespoons anchovy paste
  5 tablespoons olive oil
  2 tablespoons basil
  2 tablespoons oregano
  2 tablespoons garlic powder

Instructions

Heat a water bath to 150°.

Cook the pasta according to package directions. Drain and cool.
Place on a tea towel to remove excess moisture.

Place the cooled dry pasta (divide equally) into the 16 ounce
ramekins. Mix the tomato sauce with the garlic paste. Pour the sauce
equally among the ramekins and toss to coat the fettucine. Reserve
some of the sauce to pour on top of the chicken. Sprinkle the chicken
breasts with the garlic powder. Place the chicken on top of the
fettucine. Top with the reserved sauce followed by 3 slices of cheese
in each ramekin. Place ramekins in individual bags and pulse to seal.
Place in the water bath and cook for 3 hours.

Make the topping for the chicken. Heat the olive oil over medium heat. Add the anchovy paste and stir until it has dissolved into the oil. Add the bread crumbs and herbs. Saute until golden brown.

Remove the ramekins from the bags and top with seasoned bread crumbs. Enjoy.

Recipe Notes

The cooking times are for 1 to 1 1/2 inch thick chicken breasts.

Chicken Prosciutto Pie

- Serves: 4.
- Preparation time is 30 minutes.
- Cooking time is 3 hours.

Ingredients

12	slices prosciutto
4	4 inch spring form pans
1 1/2	tablespoons olive oil, for sauteing
1	teaspoon margarine, for sauteing
1	small onion, chopped
1	cup brown rice in a bag
1	head broccoli, cut-up
2	boneless skinless chicken breasts, cut into 1" cubes
8	ounces wild mushrooms, sliced
1	can light beer

Sauce

2	cups extra sharp cheddar cheese, shredded
4	ounces low fat cream cheese
4	basil leaf sprigs, for garnish
3/4	cup chicken stock
3	tablespoons extra sharp cheddar cheese, for garnish

Instructions

Heat a water bath to 150°.

Heat the olive oil and margarine over medium high heat in a large sauce pan. Add the mushrooms and saute until browned. Lower the heat to medium low and add the onions. Saute until translucent. Remove from heat and cool.

Remove the rice from the bag and place in the large sauce pan that was used to cook the mushrooms and onions. Prepare the rice according to directions but substitute the beer for the water. Cool.

* Place the broccoli in a microwave safe bowl with 2 tbls. water. Cover and microwave for 4 mins. on high power. Leave the broccoli in the microwave for 5 mins. after it has finished cooking. Remove from the microwave and cool.

Make the sauce by processing the cream cheese, chicken stock (add the chicken stock slowly- do not add too much as you might not need all of the 3/4 cup), and cheddar cheese in a food processor. The sauce should not be runny but quite thick.

*Line each spring form pan with three slices of prosciutto. Tear one piece in half to place on the bottom and reserve the other half for the top which will enclose the filling. Make sure there are no holes which reveal the pan. If necessary, tear small pieces of prosciutto to cover holes. Combine the rice with the sauteed mushrooms and onions. Place 1/4 rice mixture in each pan followed by 1/4 of the broccoli pieces. Equally divide the chicken pieces among the pans. Top the chicken with the sauce and place the reserved prosciutto on top. Make sure that the prosciutto completely covers everything. Place each spring form pan in an individual bag. Pulse to seal. The bag should be putting gentle pressure on top of the prosciutto. Cook for 2 hours.

Warm the serving plates in an oven. Remove the pies from the bags and plate upside down (the bottom is now right side up) onto the warmed plates. Release the spring. Remove the bottom by gently prying with a knife. Garnish by sprinkling the cheddar cheese on top followed with a sprig of basil.

Recipe Notes

WARNING THIS RECIPE CONTAINS ALCOHOL.

*You may cook the broccoli in the water bath but you must do this ahead of time. You can do it the night before. Heat a water bath to 183°. Place the broccoli in a bag and remove the air and seal. Cook for 45 mins. Make sure you deep chill the broccoli in an ice bath for 1 hour and refrigerate until ready to use in the recipe.

**Prosciutto slices vary in size so be sure you have enough.

Creamy Chicken and Wild Mushroom Casserole

- Serves: 4.
- Preparation time is 15 minutes.
- Cooking time is 2 hours.

<u>Ingredients</u>

1	small onion, chopped
2	ounces low fat cream cheese
1/2	cup Swiss cheese, shredded
1/2	cup Gruyere, shredded
1	cup cheddar cheese, shredded
1/4	cup chicken stock
2	tablespoons mayonnaise
7	ounces egg noodles
1 1/2	tablespoons grapeseed oil
20	Cheddar Cheese Almond Nut-thins, crumbled
2	16 ounce ramekins
2	chicken breast halves, boneless & skinless, cut into 1" pieces
1 1/2	tablespoons butter
1/4	cup cheddar cheese, (see instructions)
12	ounces wild mushrooms
1/4	cup Imagine mushroom soup

<u>Instructions</u>

Heat water bath to 150 °.

Heat the grape seed oil and butter over medium high heat. Add the wild mushrooms to the pan and saute until golden brown and reduced in size. Lower the heat to medium. Add the onions and saute until translucent. Remove from heat and divide the mixture into two servings and place in 16 ounce ramekins.

In a food processor, add chicken stock, mushroom soup, mayonaise, cream cheese, swiss cheese, gruyere cheese, and cheddar cheese. Process until smooth. Pour 1/2 of sauce equally over the mushroom mixture in each ramekin. Reserve the other 1/2 of sauce for finishing. Mix to combine with mushroom mixture. Place chicken on top of mixture completely covering the mixture (this acts as a barrier to prevent the sauce from overflowing the ramekin when you seal it).

Place each ramekin in an individual bag. Pulse to seal, allowing the bag to put light pressure on top of chicken. Over pulsing will result in the liquid spilling over into the bag. Place in water bath. Cook for 2 hours.

Warm four plates in the oven. You will divide the casserole into four servings. Keeping the plates warm will maintain the temperature of the casserole.

Before removing chicken from water bath, cook the egg noodles according to package directions. Divide the noodles into equal portions and place on heated plates. Remove ramekins from bags. Mix the chicken into the mushroom cream sauce mixture. Divide contents of ramekins into equal servings and place on top of egg noodles. Mix chicken and the sauce in with the egg noodles until combined. Place plates back in the lower racks of oven to keep warm. Cover plates with foil to keep from drying out.

Preheat an oven broiler on low. Spray an aluminium foil lined baking sheet with cooking spray. Mix nut thins and the 1/4 cup cheddar cheese together and place on baking sheet. Place under broiler until the cheese melts and the nut thins crisp up. Meanwhile, heat the remaining cream sauce in the microwave until warmed through. Remove the nut thin/cheddar topping from broiler. Remove the casserole plates from the bottom racks of the oven. Incorporate the warmed sauce equally onto each plate. Top with the nut thin/ cheddar topping and serve.

De-constructed Chicken Pot Pie

- Serves: 4.
- Preparation time is 10 minutes.
- Cooking time is 4 hours.

<u>Ingredients</u>

    5 tablespoons margarine
    3 chicken breasts, skinned & boned
    1 tablespoon garlic powder
    1 tablespoon dried thyme
    1 tablespoon dried rosemary
    8 ounces baby carrots, chopped
    6 ounces mushrooms thinly sliced
    8 ounces onions, chopped
    2 tablespoons chicken demi glace
1 1/2 cups chicken stock
    1 tablespoon cornstarch slurry
    4 16 ounce ramekins
    8 prepared puff pastry rounds (see recipe)

<u>Instructions</u>

Heat a water bath to 184 °.

Combine the chicken stock and demi glace in a sauce pan. Cook over medium heat. Stir until demi glace has completely melted into stock. Raise the heat to high. Add the cornstarch slurry (add more corn starch slurry if the sauce has not thickened sufficiently) and stir over high heat until incorporated and sauce has thickened. Remove from heat and cool. Divide the carrots, onions, and mushrooms equally among the 16 ounce ramekins. Divide the sauce equally among the ramekins. Do not over fill as you will be adding the cooked chicken to the vegetable mixture. Place each ramekin in an individual bag and pulse to seal. * Place in the water bath for 2 hours.

Lower the water bath to 150 °.

Cut the chicken into 1 inch pieces. Sprinkle the chicken breasts evenly with the garlic powder, thyme and rosemary. Place the chicken in a bag with the margarine. Remove the air and seal. Place in the water bath and cook for 2 hours. Make 8 rounds of puff pastry and bake as directed. Keep warm. Remove the chicken from the bags, reserving the liquid in the bag. Remove the vegetables from their bags. Combine the chicken and vegetables and divide equally into the ramekins. Stir in a little bit of the reserved liquid from the cooked chicken being careful not to make it too soupy. Place ramekins on a plate and top with one round of puff pastry. Serve the other round alongside for garnish.

Recipe Notes

*You will leave the vegetables in the water bath along with the chicken. The vegetables will not continue to cook. If you have another water oven you will be able to cook the vegetables and the chicken separately at different temperatures. This will decrease the amount of time to complete the meal by one hour or cook the chicken the night before. Cool in an ice bath for one hour and refrigerate. Thirty minutes before you serve the meal, lower the water bath from 184° to 149°. Place the cooked chicken in the water bath to reheat.

Save the reserved liquid from the chicken and use it for other sauces. If you make extra chicken/vegetables use it to serve on top of fettuccine for another dinner.

The cooking time is for 1 to 1 1/2 inch thick chicken breasts.

Italian Chicken Zucchini Bundles

- Serves: 4.
- Preparation time is 15 minutes.
- Cooking time is 4 1/2 hours.

<u>Ingredients</u>

4	4" dia. spring form pans
6	large zucchini, 1/4" thick slice lengthwise
40	slices pepperoni, 2" diameter
4	medium tomatoes, sliced
1	teaspoon basil
1	teaspoon oregano
1	tablespoon garlic powder
1 1/2	boneless skinless chicken breast halves, (12 ounces) cut into 1" cubes
8	ounces Asiago cheese, sliced

<u>Sauce</u>

1	small onion, chopped
1	tablespoon olive oil, for sauteing
4	ounces low fat cream cheese
1	tablespoon tomato paste
1/2	cup chicken stock
1	cup Parmesan cheese, grated
1	fresh basil leaves, for garnish

<u>Instructions</u>

Heat a water bath to 184°.

Place the zucchini slices in a bag. Remove the air and seal. Place in the water bath and cook for 2 hours. Remove the zucchini from bags and allow to cool.

Lower the water bath to 150°.

Line the bottom of each spring form pan with 5 slices of pepperoni. Using two zucchini slices, place them along the sides of the spring form pans forming a circle. Make sure the slices overlap. Place a couple of slices of tomatoes in each pan and sprinkle with the basil and oregano. Put half of the Asiago slices on top of the tomatoes. Place three zucchini slices (on top of the tomatoes) in each pan allowing them to overlap each other and are protruding outside of the pan. They will be folded over on top of the next layer of ingredients. Portion out the chicken pieces, (which have been sprinkled with garlic powder) and place on top of the zucchini. Top with the remaining Asiago cheese slices. Now fold the zucchini that was over hanging the pan on top of the chicken cheese mixture. Place five more pepperoni slices on top making sure to completely cover the top. Place each ramekin in an individual bag and pulse to seal. The bag should be pressing lightly down on top of the pepperoni. Place in the water bath and cook for a minimum of 2 1/2 hours.

For the sauce, saute the onions in olive oil over medium heat until translucent. Make a well in the middle of the sauce pan and add the tomato paste. Heat the tomato paste over low heat. Allow the paste to lightly brown. Add the chicken stock and the cream cheese. Continue to heat over low until the cream cheese has melted. Add the Parmesan cheese. Keep warm.

Remove the spring form pans from the bags and place upside down (the bottom of the pan will now be right side up) on a warmed plate. Release the pan and remove. Remove the bottom by gently using a knife to pry off. Spoon the sauce on top. Garnish with fresh basil.

Lemon Chicken

- Serves: 2.
- Preparation time is 20 minutes.
- Cooking time is 3 1/2 hours.

Ingredients

      2 chicken breasts, boneless & skinless, cut into 1/2" cubes
      6 ounces mushrooms thinly sliced
      1 lemon, sliced thin
      2 tablespoons lemon zest
    10 new potatoes, cubed
      4 tablespoons margarine
      6 ounces artichoke hearts, halved
      6 slices bacon, cooked
      4 ounces low fat cream cheese
    1/4 cup chicken stock
  1 1/2 tablespoons garlic paste
      8 ounces Parmesan cheese, grated
      2 16 ounce ramekins

Instructions

Heat a water bath to 185°.

Place the cubed potatoes in a bag with the lemon zest (from the
lemon you will slice). Add the lemon slices, grated parmesan and 2
tbls. margarine. Remove the air and seal. Place in the water bath.
Cook for 2 hours.

Heat the remaining 2 tbls. of margarine over high heat. Immediately
add the mushrooms and saute until golden brown. Remove from heat
and allow to cool.

Lower the bath after the potatoes have cooked to 150°. Keep the
cooked potatoes in the water bath while the chicken is cooking. Make
the sauce in the blender by processing the cream cheese, garlic paste,
and the chicken stock. Process until well combined.

Equally divided the chicken into each ramekin followed by the cooled
mushrooms. Pour the sauce equally over the chicken. Mix all the
ingredients until well combined. Place each ramekin in a bag and

pulse to seal. Place in the water bath and cook for a minimum of 1 1/2 hours.

Heat a (regular) oven to 180°. The lemon chicken will be served in pasta bowls. Put the bowls in the oven to keep warm. Cook the bacon. Keep the bacon warm in the oven. Drain the artichokes and place on a plate to keep warm in the oven also.

Drain the potatoes by clipping off one edge of the bag. Allow the liquid to drain. Discard the liquid or reserve for another use. Remove the potatoes from the bag. Portion out the potatoes into the warmed pasta bowls. Remove the ramekins from the bags. Stir the chicken garlic sauce into the potatoes. Add the warmed artichokes and top with the bacon. Serve.

Recipe Notes

If by a small chance there are any leftovers, serve cold over bibb lettuce for another meal.

Orange Garlic Five Spice Injected Chicken

- Serves: 4.
- Preparation time is 10 minutes.
- Cooking time is 3 hours.

Ingredients

4 tablespoons margarine, melted
2 tablespoons garlic powder
2 tablespoons chinese five spice
2 oranges, zested & juiced
4 large chicken breasts, bone-in
4 tablespoons margarine, for the bags

Instructions

Heat a water bath to 150°.

Combine the orange juice, melted butter, garlic, zest and chinese five spice. Using a food injector, draw up the liquid. Lift the skin of the chicken breasts (it is important not to pierce the skin as the skin acts as a barrier that keeps the marinade within the chicken) and insert the injector into various spots throughout the breasts. You will notice the breasts will puff up. Place each breast in an individual bag and top with 1 tbls. of margarine. Seal the bag by gently pulsing just until the bag begins to press down on the chicken. *Place in a water bath and cook for 3 hours.

Remove the chicken from the bag and reserve the liquid. You may use the liquid as an au jus for your chicken. Crisp the skin by using a kitchen torch or place under a broiler.

Recipe Notes

*The cooking time is for 1 1/2 inch thick chicken breasts.

Pheasant with Orange Madeira Sauce

- Serves: 2.
- Preparation time is 15 minutes.
- Inactive preparation time is 15 minutes.
- Cooking time is 5 hours.

Ingredients

        4 tablespoons margarine
    2 1/2 pounds 2 pheasants, breast removed from bone
            Sauce
      1/2 cup madeira
        1 orange, juiced
        2 tablespoons chicken demi glace
      1/2 cup chicken stock

Instructions

Heat a water bath to 140°.

Debone the pheasants by removing the breast bone and the back bone or ask your butcher to do it for you. Place each pheasant in an individual bag with 2 tbls. each of margarine. Remove the air and seal. Place in the water bath and cook for five hours.

Make the sauce a half an hour prior to serving. Heat the Madeira and the orange juice and reduce by half. * Add the demi glace and the chicken stock and reduce until consistency of sauce thickens.

Remove the pheasants from the bags and place on a baking sheet. **Sear pheasants with a cooking torch until skin has browned and crisped. Spoon the sauce on top of the pheasants and serve.

Recipe Notes

WARNING THIS RECIPE CONTAINS ALCOHOL.

*Use cornstarch to thicken sauce if desired.

**It is not recommended to sear the pheasants under the broiler. This would cause them to dry out.

Tandoori Chicken with Raita Sauce

- Serves: 4.
- Preparation time is 15 minutes.
- Inactive preparation time is 4 hours.
- Cooking time is 4 hours.

Ingredients

```
       4  pounds whole chickens, cut in pieces and skin removed
     1/2  cup onion, chopped
       2  tablespoons garlic paste
       2  tablespoons ginger, chopped
       1  teaspoon jalapeno pepper, stem and seeds removed
       1  tablespoon paprika
   1 1/2  teaspoons salt
       1  teaspoon cumin
       1  teaspoon tumeric
       1  teaspoon coriander, ground
       1  teaspoon garam masala
     1/2  teaspoon cayenne pepper
     1/2  cup Plain nonfat Greek yogurt
       1  tablespoon lemon juice
          Raita Sauce
       1  cup Plain nonfat Greek yogurt
       1  tablespoon cilantro, chopped
       1  tablespoon fresh mint, chopped
       1  teaspoon cumin
       1  small seedless cucumber, peeled & finely diced
```

Instructions

Prick holes with a fork in the chicken pieces. Cut diagonal slits 1 inch apart and 1/2 inch deep in the larger pieces of chicken. Place the chicken pieces in a bag.

Make the marinade by combining the onion, garlic, ginger, and jalapeno in a blender and process on high speed until well blended. Add the paprika, salt, cumin, turmeric, coriander, garam masala, and cayenne. Process until well combined. Next, add the yogurt and the fresh lemon juice and process until the sauce is smooth. Pour the marinade in the bag with the chicken. Make sure the sauce is coating all of the chicken. Seal the bag (it is not necessary to remove all of the air at this point). Refrigerate for a minimum of 4 hours or overnight.

Make the Raita sauce. Peel the cucumbers and finely dice them. Place the cucumbers on a tea towel. Lightly salt them and allow them to set for 5 minutes on the towel. Squeeze the juice out of the cucumbers by wringing the tea towel. Combine the Greek yogurt, cucumbers, cilantro, mint, and cumin. Refrigerate until ready to serve.

Heat a water bath to 151°.

Remove the chicken from the marinade and pat dry. Heat the grapeseed oil over high heat in a large skillet. Wait until you see the oil rippling, and add a few pieces of chicken at a time. Brown on all sides. Remove the chicken and place on a plate to cool. Place in the refrigerator covered in plastic wrap until you are ready to cook. Place the chicken pieces in a bag and seal removing the air. Place the bag in a water bath and cook for 4 hours.

Remove the chicken from the bags and plate. Top the chicken with the Raita sauce and serve.

Yummy Turkey Breast

- Serves: 4.
- Preparation time is 5 minutes.
- Inactive preparation time is 5 minutes.
- Cooking time is 4 1/2 hours.

Ingredients

     5 pounds turkey breast, divided in 1/2 & bone removed
    1/2 cup chicken stock
     1 package onion soup mix
     4 tablespoons margarine
     2 cups chicken stock
     2 tablespoons kitchen bouquet
        cornstarch, for thickening

Instructions

Place a 1/4 cup each of chicken stock into two bags. Make sure the bags are large enough to hold one half of the turkey breast each. Seal but do not remove the air. Place in the freezer until frozen. This can be done the night before.

Heat a water bath to 150°.

Divide the onion soup mix in half and rub into each turkey breast. Remove the bags containing the frozen stock from the freezer. Place one breast in each bag. Top each breast with 2 tbls. margarine. Remove the air and seal the bag. Cook for 4 hours.

Remove turkey from water oven. Slit open a small portion of the top of the bag and pour the liquid out of the bag and reserve. Seal the bag again (it is not necessary to remove the air) and place back in the water bath to keep warm while you are making the gravy.

Combine the reserved liquid from the bags with the 2 cups chicken stock and the kitchen bouquet. *Thicken the gravy by making a cornstarch slurry. Keep warm. Remove turkey from bags and sear the skin with a kitchen torch or place under a preheated broiler to brown skin. Serve.

<u>Recipe Notes</u>

The cooking time is for 2 inch thick turkey breasts.

*To make a cornstarch slurry, combine equal parts cornstarch with cold water. Stir until dissolved. Whisk the slurry in small amounts into gravy until desired consistency is achieved.

Seafood

Flounder Stuffed with Crabmeat   143
Garlic Ginger Fish with Shitake Mushroom Soy Glaze   145
Halibut a la Parmesan   146
Jambalaya   148
Lobster   149
Lobster Newburg   150
Poblanos stuffed with Chorizo and Shrimp   152
Red Grouper Poached in Butter Sauce   154
Red Snapper Vera Cruz   155
Seafood Cioppino   156
Seafood Lasagne   158
Shrimp & Sausage   160
Shrimp Caesar Pizza   161
Spanish Paella   162
Tuna Casserole   164

Cooking Tables For Seafood

TIMES ARE FOR THAWED NOT FROZEN SEAFOOD

ADD 30 MINIMUM COOKING TIMES

SEAFOOD	THICKNESS (INCHES)	TEMPERATURE	COOKING TIMES (MINIMUM TIME)
FISH	½	140°	30 MINUTES
FISH	1	140°	45 MINUTES
FISH	1 ½	140°	1 HOUR
SCALLOPS (DIVER)	1	140°	40 MINUTES
LOBSTER	-	143°	45 MINUTES
SHRIMP	-	143°	30 MINUTES
MUSSELS	-	143°	40 MINUTES
CLAMS	-	143°	40 MINUTES

Flounder Stuffed with Crabmeat

- Serves: 2.
- Preparation time is 15 minutes.
- Cooking time is 2 hours and 45 minutes.

Ingredients

    1/3 red pepper, finely diced
    1/3 yellow pepper, finely diced
    1/3 green pepper, finely diced
    1/3 small onion, finely diced
    1/4 cup Blue Diamond ranch nut thins, ground
      1 cup lump crab meat
      1 teaspoon Old Bay seasoning
      1 tablespoon dijon mustard
1 1/2 tablespoons Worcestershire sauce
1 1/2 tablespoons mayonnaise
      1 pound flounder filets
         Sauce
    1/4 cup chicken stock
      4 ounces low fat cream cheese
      1 cup Parmesan cheese, grated
1 1/2 tablespoons lemon juice
      2 tablespoons capers

Instructions

Heat a water bath to 182°.

*Put all of the vegetables in a bag. Remove the air and seal. Place in the water bath and cook for 2 hours. Remove from the bag and cool.

Lower the water bath to 140°.

Combine the cooled vegetables with the mayonnaise, ground nut thins, dijon, old bay, and worcestershire sauce. Carefully fold in the crabmeat. ** Place one fillet flat inside a bag. Spoon crab/vegetable mixture on top. Place the other fillet on top of the crab mixture. Seal by pulsing the machine until the bag fits tightly around the fish. Over pulsing may crush the fish. Place in the water bath and cook for 45 minutes.

Meanwhile, make the sauce. Heat the chicken stock over medium heat. Add the cream cheese and lemon juice. When sauce is heated through and cream cheese is dissolved into stock, lower the heat and slowly add the Parmesan cheese. Keep stirring until cheese is melted. Add the capers. Keep warm.

Heat the serving plates in a warm oven. Remove the fish from bags by cutting along the sides of the bag and sliding the fish onto the warmed plate. Divide into portions. Spoon the sauce on top of the fish and enjoy.

Recipe Notes

*The vegetables may be cooked a day ahead. Place them in an ice bath after cooking for a 1/2 hour and refrigerate.

**Try to get two fillets similar in size. This will enable you to enclose the filling. This recipe is for 1/2 inch thick fillets.

Garlic Ginger Fish w/ Shitake Mushroom Soy Glaze

- Serves: 4.
- Preparation time is 15 minutes.
- Cooking time is 1 hour.

Ingredients

    3   tablespoons canola oil, for sauteing
    2   pounds cod fillets
    2   bunches scallions, chopped
   20   ounces shitake mushrooms, stems removed & sliced
        garlic powder, to sprinkle
        ginger, to sprinkle
        Sauce
    2   tablespoons red wine vinegar
  1/2   cup soy sauce

Instructions

Heat a water bath to 140°.

Saute the mushrooms over medium high heat. After the mushrooms have browned, add the scallions and saute for 1 minute or until softened. Set aside and cool.

Make the sauce by combining the red wine vinegar and the soy sauce.

Sprinkle the fish with the garlic and ginger on one side of fish. Place the fillets in a bag and pour the sauce on top. Place the cooled scallions and mushrooms on top. Remove the air and seal. Place in the water bath. Cook for 1 hour.

Recipe Notes

The cod fillets should be 1 inch thick.

Halibut a la Parmesan

- Serves: 4.
- Preparation time is 5 minutes.
- Cooking time is 45 minutes.

Ingredients

2 pounds halibut, cut in half
6 tablespoons mayonnaise
12 dashes hot sauce
2 bunches scallions, thinly sliced
2 tablespoons lemon juice
1 cup Parmesan cheese, grated
1/2 cup bread crumbs
2/3 tablespoon anchovy paste
2/3 tablespoon basil
2/3 tablespoon oregano
2/3 tablespoon garlic powder

Instructions

Heat a water bath to 140°.

In a mixing bowl combine the mayonnaise, hot sauce, lemon juice, Parmesan, and scallions.

Place the fish in a bag and top each fillet with the mayonnaise mixture. Pulse to seal the fish. Place in a water bath and cook for 45 minutes.

Meanwhile, make the topping by heating the olive oil over medium heat. Add the anchovy paste and stir until it has dissolved into the oil. Add the bread crumbs and spices. Continue to saute until the bread crumbs are golden brown.

Warm the serving plates in the oven.

Remove the fish from the bag by cutting down the sides of the bag and top and peel back. Using a spatula gently lift the fish onto the heated plate. Top the fish with the bread crumbs. Serve.

Recipe Notes

The thickness of the fish should be 1 inch.

Jambalaya

- Serves: 4.
- Preparation time is 10 minutes.
- Inactive preparation time is 10 minutes.
- Cooking time is 3 hours.

Ingredients

    2 boneless skinless chicken breasts, cut 1" thick pieces
    2 andouille sausages, cut into 1/4" thick slices
    2 pints grape tomatoes
 1/4 cup chicken stock
    2 tablespoons margarine
    2 cups brown rice
2 1/2 cups chicken stock
 1/2 pound shrimp, shells removed
    2 bunches scallions, thinly sliced

Instructions

Heat a water bath to 151°.

Freeze the 1/4 cup chicken stock in a bag large enough to later hold the chicken, sausage, and tomatoes. When liquid is frozen, place the afore mentioned ingredients in the bag. Top with 2 tbls. margarine. Seal and place in the water bath. Cook for 3 hours.

*Cook the rice according to package directions but substitute chicken stock for water. The last three minutes of cooking time for the rice, add the** shrimp and scallions (reserve some scallions for garnish). When the rice is ready, pour onto a heated serving plater. Top off the rice with the jambalaya and sprinkle with the scallions.

Recipe Notes

**You may sous vide the shrimp but you will have to lower the water bath temperature to 143° after the chicken/sausage mixture has cooked. Leave the chicken/sausage in the bath while you are cooking the shrimp. Cook the shrimp for 1/2 an hour.

*Success Brown Rice in a bag was used for this recipe. The rice was removed from the bag.

Lobster

- Serves: 4.
- Preparation time is 10 minutes.
- Cooking time is 45 minutes.

Ingredients

    4 lobster tail
    8 tablespoons butter

Instructions

Heat a water bath to 143°.

Thaw the lobster tails if they are frozen. Remove the shells. This is easily done if you use kitchen shears and cut down the length of the shell on both sides. Place tails in a bag with the butter. Remove the air by pulsing and seal. Cook for 45 minutes.

Serve with melted butter and fresh lemon.

Lobster Newburg

- Serves: 4.
- Preparation time is 15 minutes.
- Inactive preparation time is 15 minutes.
- Cooking time is 45 minutes.

Ingredients

9	ounces mushrooms thinly sliced
1/2	green pepper, finely diced
1	small onion, finely chopped
2	tablespoons butter, for sauteing
1/2	cup chicken stock
1/4	teaspoon nutmeg
1/2	teaspoon cayenne pepper
1 1/2	tablespoons garlic, minced
1/4	cup dry sherry, plus 4 tbls.
10	ounces low fat cream cheese
2	ounces frozen peas
15	ounces lobster tail, cut into 1" pieces
1	9"x5"glass loaf pan
7 1/2	ounces fettuccine

Instructions

Heat a water bath to 143°.

Saute the mushrooms in 1 tbls. butter over high heat until browned. Lower the heat to medium and add the onions and green pepper. Saute until softened. Add the minced garlic, cayenne pepper, and nutmeg and saute until cooked through (approximately 2 mins.). Add the sherry and cook until almost completely evaporated. Add the chicken stock and cook until it has warmed. Lower the heat and add the low fat cream cheese. Stir until cheese is completely melted into the sauce. Remove from heat and allow to cool.

Remove the lobster from shells and cut into 1/2" pieces. Pour the cooled sauce into the loaf pan. Add the lobster meat and gently mix until combined. Place the loaf pan in an 11" wide bag and pulse to seal. Place in water bath for 45 minutes.

Heat an oven to 180°. Place the pasta bowls in the oven to keep warm. Allow the frozen peas to come to room temp or place in oven 5 mins. before serving.

Right before serving, cook the pasta according to directions. Place the cooked pasta into the warmed pasta bowls. Remove the loaf pan from the bag and spoon the sauce on top of the pasta. Sprinkle with peas. Serve.

Recipe Notes

WARNING THIS RECIPE CONTAINS ALCOHOL.

This recipe has a little zip. If less heat is desired, cut the cayenne pepper down to 1/4 teaspoon.

For a variation of this recipe try serving over puff pastry.

Poblanos stuffed with Chorizo and Shrimp

- Serves: 4.
- Preparation time is 20 minutes.
- Inactive preparation time is 20 minutes.
- Cooking time is 45 minutes.

Ingredients

2	large poblano chiles
1/2	pound shrimp, shelled
2	cans Rotel diced tomatoes w/green chiles, drained
1/2	small onion, sliced
1	tablespoon margarine, for sauteing
1/2	pound Mexican Chorizo
3/4	cup sharp cheddar cheese, shredded
3/4	cup monterey jack, shredded
1	cup brown rice in a bag
1 1/4	cups chicken stock
4	6 inch plates

Instructions

Preheat oven to 400°.

Preheat a water bath to 150°.

*Remove the rice from the bag and cook rice according to package directions in the chicken stock. Let cool. Saute the onions in the margarine until translucent. Cool.

Cut the poblanos in half and remove the stems, seeds, and veins. Place on a baking sheet and bake in the 400° oven for 20 to 30 minutes or until poblanos are completely cooked. Let cool. Place two polblano halves on each of the two six inch plates. Heat a regular oven to 180°. Place the other two plates in the oven to keep warm.

Cut the shelled shrimp into 1/2 inch pieces. Remove the casings from the chorizo and mince. Mix together the rice, shrimp, Rotel tomatoes, onions and sausage. Spoon the rice on top of the poblanos. Equally divide the cheese and top each poblano. Place the two plates in individual bags and pulse to seal. Place in the water bath and cook for 45 minutes. Remove the poblanos on the plates from the bags by cutting away the sides of the bags. Portion the poblanos and place on the two plates that were kept warm in the oven. One poblano half per serving.

Recipe Notes

*Success Brown Rice in a bag was used for this recipe.

Red Grouper poached in Butter Sauce

- Serves: 2.
- Preparation time is 5 minutes.
- Cooking time is 50 minutes.

Ingredients

      6 ounces mushrooms thinly sliced
      5 tablespoons margarine
  1/2 lemon, sliced 1/4" thick
   16 ounces red grouper fillet, divided into two portions

Instructions

Heat a water bath to 140°.

Saute the mushrooms in 1 tbls. butter until golden brown. Cool.

Place each fillet in an individual bag. Equally divide the lemon and mushrooms and place on top of the fillets. Top with 2 tbls. each margarine. Pulse to seal so that the fish will not be crushed. Cook for 50 minutes.

Recipe Notes

You may substitute the grouper for halibut or any other firm thick fish. Thin fillets such as tilapia will not work for this recipe.

Red Snapper Vera Cruz

- Serves: 4.
- Preparation time is 5 minutes.
- Cooking time is 2 hours and 40 minutes.

Ingredients

    2 small onions, thinly sliced
    2 cans green chili peppers, diced
  32 kalamata olives
    1 pound feta cheese, cut into 1/2" cubes
    2 tablespoons margarine
  12 tomatoes, sliced
     garlic powder, for sprinkling
    4 red snapper fillets, skin removed, 1" thickness

Instructions

Heat a water bath to 182°.

Place the tomatoes, onions, green chiles and butter in a bag. Remove the air and seal. Cook for 2 hours.

Lower the water bath to 140°. Leave the vegetables in the water bath to keep warm. Sprinkle the garlic powder on top of one side of the fish and top with the olives. Place in a bag. Remove the air by pulsing and seal. Cook for 40 minutes.

Keep the plates warm in an oven. Remove the fish from bag and place on plates. Top with the tomato, green chile sauce and feta cheese.

Recipe Notes

Any fish can be used in this recipe. Adjust cooking times for the thickness of the fish.

Seafood Cioppino

- Serves: 4.
- Preparation time is 10 minutes.
- Cooking time is 40 minutes.

Ingredients

1	small onion, chopped
1/2	green pepper, chopped
1 1/2	tablespoons garlic, minced
1 1/2	teaspoons red pepper flakes
14	ounces crushed tomatoes
6	ounces tomato sauce
1 1/2	cups dry white wine
1	tablespoon basil
1	tablespoon oregano
1	teaspoon dried thyme
20	mussels
1/2	pound cod fillet, cut into 1" cubes
20	shrimp, shells removed
20	scallops
8	ounces clams, canned, minced
3	tablespoons margarine
1	tablespoon garlic paste
1	tablespoon margarine
2	16 ounce ramekins
2	tablespoons olive oil, for sauteing
1	cup lemon basil leaf, chiffonade

Instructions

Heat a water bath to 143°.

In a bowl, mix the 3 Tbls. margarine with the garlic paste. *Clean the mussels and remove the beards. Place the mussels, equally divided, into the ramekins. Top with the garlic butter. Place each ramekin in an individual bag. Pulse to seal, allowing the bag to just put a little pressure on top of the mussels. If you seal it too tightly the mussels will not have enough room to open. Place in the water bath. Cook for 40 minutes.

Drain the clams and reserve the liquid for the broth. Place the clams, shrimp, scallops, and cod pieces in a bag. Top the seafood with 1 Tbls. margarine. Pulse to seal and place in the water bath. Cook for 30 minutes.

Meanwhile, make the sauce. In a large deep skillet, saute the onions and green pepper in the olive oil over medium heat. Add the garlic and red pepper flakes and cook for 1 minute. Add half of the wine and the basil, oregano, and thyme. Simmer until the wine has reduced by half. Stir in the tomato sauce, crushed tomatoes, and reserved clam juice. Simmer on low for 5 minutes. Add the rest of the wine and continue to simmer on low for another 5 minutes. Cover skillet and keep broth warm.

Add the mussels with the garlic butter to the broth. Add the seafood with the liquid to the broth. Gently stir to incorporate. Place the cover back on the skillet and allow the flavors to meld for 5 minutes. The heat should still be on warm.

Spoon the cioppino into pasta bowls and top with the **lemon basil. Serve.

Recipe Notes

WARNING THIS RECIPE CONTAINS ALCOHOL.

*You may substitute frozen, pasteurized mussels for fresh mussels. This is recommended for those who are immune compromised or are in ill health.

**Plain basil may be substituted. Squeeze the juice of a fresh lemon over the broth before serving.

The cooking times are for 1 inch thick scallops, cod fillets and large shrimp.

Seafood Lasagne

- Serves: 2.
- Preparation time is 15 minutes.
- Inactive preparation time is 15 minutes.
- Cooking time is 45 minutes.

Ingredients

1/3	pound shrimp, peeled and devined
1	lobster tail, cut in chunks
4	brown rice lasagne noodles, cooked
8	ounces lump crab meat, drained
1	small onion, chopped
1	tablespoon margarine
3	ounces capers
1	tablespoon lemon juice
16	ounces Parmesan sauce, see recipe
2	16 ounce ramekins
10	large lemon basil leaves, chiffonade

Instructions

Heat a water bath to 143°.

Melt the margarine in a skillet. Add the onions and cook until translucent. Remove from heat and let cool.

Prepare Parmesan sauce according to directions. Add lemon juice to sauce and incorporate.

Cook lasagna noodles according to package directions. Place on a tea towel to dry and cool.

Pour a little Parmesan sauce into the bottom of the ramekins. Add one noodle which has been cut in 1/2 to the bottom of each ramekin. The noodles will not be a perfect fit but will overlap and go up the side of the dish. Pour in 1/2 of Parmesan sauce mixture, equally divided, into each ramekin. Mix in the onions, capers, shrimp, lobster and crab. Top with the remaining noodles which again have been cut in 1/2. Top with the remaining Parmesan sauce. Place each ramekin in an individual bag and pulse to seal. Cook for 45 minutes. Remove from bags and put ramekins on top of a plate to serve. *Top lasagna with lemon basil to garnish.

Recipe Notes

*You may substitute fresh basil and the zest of a lemon for the lemon basil.

Shrimp & Sausage

- Serves: 4.
- Preparation time is 5 minutes.
- Cooking time is 30 minutes.

Ingredients

    2 pounds shrimp with shells on
    2 tablespoons Old Bay seasoning
    2 pounds polish-style sausages, cut in chunks
    2 tablespoons margarine

Instructions

Heat a water bath to 143°.

Place the shrimp and the sausage in a bag. Add the seasoning and coat well. Add the margarine evenly placed throughout the bag. Remove the air by pulsing and seal. Place in the water bath for a 1/2 hour.

Recipe Notes

The polish sausages should be already cooked not raw.

Shrimp Caesar Pizza

- Serves: 2.
- Cooking time is 30 minutes.

Ingredients

    1/2 pound shrimp, peeled
      1 small onion, thinly sliced
      1 yellow pepper, diced
      2 tablespoons olive oil
    10 slices Provolone cheese
      4 slices bacon, cooked
      6 tablespoons caesar salad dressing
      1 bunch lemon basil leaf, chiffonade
      2 brown rice tortilla

Instructions

Preheat a water bath to 143°.

Place peeled shrimp into a bag. Remove the air by pulsing and seal.
Place in the water bath and cook for 30 mins.

Meanwhile, place a pizza stone or a wire dehydrating rack on the lower
rack in the oven and preheat to 485°. Saute the onions and the
yellow pepper in olive oil until soft. Place 5 slices of provolone cheese
on each tortilla and top with the caesar dressing. Top with the
onion/pepper mixture and crumbled slices of the cooked bacon. Place
on top of the rack/stone and bake for 10 minutes or until cheese has
melted and lightly browned.

Remove the shrimp from the water bath and top the cooked pizza.
Garnish with the lemon basil. Serve.

Spanish Paella

- Serves: 8.
- Preparation time is 10 minutes.
- Cooking time is 3 hours and 40 minutes.

Ingredients

1	tablespoon smoked paprika
2	teaspoons oregano
2	pounds boneless skinless chicken breasts, cut into 2" cubes
4	cups spanish style short grain rice
1	pinch of saffron threads
1	onion, chopped
1	red bell pepper, coarsely chopped
1	package chorizo sausage, casings removed and crumbled
1 1/2	pounds shrimp, peeled
1	pound frozen mussels in garlic butter
4	tablespoons olive oil
1	tablespoon butter
1	bay leaf
1/2	bunch flat leaf parsley, chopped
2	lemons, zested
1	bunch chives, chopped

Instructions

Heat a water bath to 150°.

If you have another water oven, heat the water to 143°. If you do not, you will lower the temperature to 143° after the chicken and the sausage have been fully cooked. Leave the chicken and sausage in the water bath to stay warm while you cook the seafood.

Saute the onions and red bell pepper in two tbls. olive oil. Cook until onions are translucent and red pepper is softened. Remove from heat and allow to cool.

Place the chicken pieces in a bag with the smoked paprika and oregano making sure to coat all of the pieces. Remove the air and seal. Place in the 150° water bath for 3 hours.

Place the crumbled sausage into a bag and add the cooled red bell pepper, and onions. Remove the air and seal. Place in the 150° water bath with the chicken. The sausage is cooking at the same time as the chicken for 3 hours.

* Place the mussels in a 16 ounce ramekin and pulse to seal. The bag should just begin to put light pressure on top of the mussels. Place the ramekin in a 143° water bath (lower the water bath temperature if you are using one water oven, after the chicken and sausage has cooked for 3 hours) and cook for 40 minutes. *Place the shrimp in a bag with the butter and pulse to seal. Place shrimp in the 143° water bath and cook for 30 minutes.

Prepare the rice 30 minutes before serving. Heat the olive oil in a large skillet over medium heat. Stir in the rice and cook for 2 minutes. Add the chicken stock, bay leaf, lemon zest and parsley. Stir well. Cover the skillet with a tight fitting lid and cook for 20 to 25 minutes. **If you are not ready to serve the rice place it (covered) in a warm oven until ready to serve.

Plate the rice on a large serving platter. Place the other ingredients on top. Garnish with chopped chives.

Recipe Notes

*If you have one oven allow additional time for cooking. The seafood must be cooked at a lower temperature than the chicken and the sausage. Do not overcook the seafood. Seafood will be come to soft if allowed to cook longer then times suggested.

**If you have two ovens you should have enough room to cook the rice ahead of time and place it in a bag. Remove the air and seal. Put the rice in the water bath to keep warm.

Tuna Casserole

- Serves: 2.
- Preparation time is 20 minutes.
- Cooking time is 1 hour.

Ingredients

    1/2 cup chicken stock
      8 ounces low fat cream cheese
1 1/2 tablespoons porcini powder
      3 tablespoons mayonnaise
      1 medium onion, chopped
      1 tablespoon olive oil, for sauteing
4 1/2 ounces wild mushrooms
      6 ounces tuna in olive oil
      4 ounces green chilies, diced
    1/2 cup extra sharp cheddar cheese, shredded
      6 ounces egg noodles
      2 16 ounce ramekins
    1/2 cup potato chip, crumbled

Instructions

Heat a water bath to 165°.

In a small sauce pan, combine the chicken stock with the porcini powder. Bring to a boil and reduce down to a simmer. Cook for 3 minutes. Add the low fat cream cheese (over low heat) and stir until completely melted. Add the mayonnaise. Remove from heat and allow to cool.

Saute the onions in the olive oil until soft and translucent. Remove from heat and allow to cool.

Cook the noodles according to package directions. Slightly under cook the noodles as they will cook a little more when placed in the water bath. Allow the noodles to cool and dry by placing on a tea towel. Mix the noodles into the sauce. Add the green chilies, mushrooms, onions, and drained tuna.

Pour mixture into ramekins. Divide the cheese sauce evenly among the ramekins. Place each ramekin in an individual bag and pulse to seal. Place in the water bath for 1 hour.

Remove ramekins from the bags and garnish with crumbled potato chips. Serve and enjoy.

Side Dishes

Asparagus   167
Blue Cheese Coleslaw   168
Boursin Gallet   169
Brandied Butter Mushrooms   170
Brussels Sprouts   171
Butternut Squash Casserole   172
Cabbage   174
Cheddar Broccoli & Rice Casserole   175
Dressings and Stuffing   176
Espuma Wasabi Potatoes   177
Fennel & Onion a la Parmesan   179
Fingerling Potatoes   180
Goat Cheese Cheesecake with Beets   181
Goody Gouda Polenta   183
Green Chile Mac & Cheese   184
Gruyere Scalloped Potatoes w/Champagne Sauce   185
Kicked Up Corn on the Cob   187
Lemon Potatoes   188
Lemon Tarragon Potato Salad   189
Mexican Rice   190
Orange Liqueur Cranberries   191
Parmesan Truffle Fries   192
Red Bliss Potatoes with Onions   193
Rutabaga Souffle   194
Savory Mushroom Strata   196
Spicy Green Beans   198
Tomato Confit   199
Vegetable Medley Casserole   200
Zucchini Towers   201

Asparagus

- Serves: 4.
- Preparation time is 5 minutes.
- Cooking time is 5 minutes.

Ingredients

    2 bunches asparagus
    2 tablespoons garlic
    4 tablespoons butter

Instructions

Bring a pot with water up to a soft boil.

Clean the asparagus and chop of the tough ends. * Place the asparagus in a bag with the butter and garlic. Remove the air and seal. Place the bag in boiling water and submerge with a plate. Cook for 5 minutes and remove the pot from heat. Keep in the warm water for up to 20 minutes.

Recipe Notes

*Minced garlic in a jar was used for this recipe. Do not use raw garlic.

Blue Cheese Coleslaw

- Serves: 4.
- Preparation time is 5 minutes.

Ingredients

1 package coleslaw mix
2 cups mayonnaise
4 tablespoons horseradish
8 ounces blue cheese, crumbled

Instructions

Place all of the ingredients in a mixing bowl and combine well. Refrigerate until ready to serve.

Boursin Gallet

- Serves: 4.
- Preparation time is 15 minutes.
- Cooking time is 2 hours and 15 minutes.

Ingredients

    1 medium red bliss potato, sliced 1/4" thick
    2 tablespoons duck fat
    4 ounces low fat cream cheese
    4 ounces boursin cheese
    1 egg
    4 ounces pineapples, cubed
    4 4" dia. spring form pans

Instructions

Heat a water bath to 165°.

In a food processor, combine the boursin and low fat cheese. Mix well. Add the egg and process until well incorporated. Divide the cheese mixture evenly among the spring form pans. Place each pan in an individual bag and pulse to seal. Place in the water bath and cook for two hours.

To make the gallet, heat a large skillet over medium high heat. Add the duck fat. Place just enough potato slices into the skillet so that they cover the bottom of the skillet. Flip the slices over so that they are lightly browned on both sides. After both sides have browned, lower the heat to low. Cover the skillet with a tight fitting lid and cook for 5 minutes. Remove the lid. Flip the potatoes over to the other side and place the lid back on and cook for another 3 to 5 minutes. Remove the cover and cook until the potatoes are completely cooked through. Remove the potatoes from the pan and place the potatoes in a circle (overlapping) on a salad plate. The circle of potatoes should be about the same size as the spring form pans and will resemble a pancake. Place the plates in a warm oven (180°) until ready to serve. Remove the spring form pans from the bags. Invert the pans onto the gallets. Remove the pan by releasing the spring form mechanism and pry the bottom off carefully with a knife. Place the cubed pineapples on top and serve.

Brandied Butter Mushrooms

- Serves: 4.
- Preparation time is 15 minutes.
- Inactive preparation time is 15 minutes.
- Cooking time is 30 minutes.

Ingredients

    16 ounces baby portabello mushroom, cleaned
    1/2 cup brandy
      4 tablespoons butter
      1 16 ounce ramekin

Instructions

Heat a water bath to 183°.

Heat the brandy in a sauce pan and cook until reduced by half. Let the sauce cool.

Place the mushrooms in a ramekin and add the cooled brandy and the butter. Place the ramekin into a large bag. Pulse to seal and place in the water bath. Cook for 1/2 hour. Remove and serve.

Recipe Notes

WARNING THIS RECIPE CONTAINS ALCOHOL.

Brussels Sprouts

- Serves: 4.
- Preparation time is 5 minutes.
- Cooking time is 1 hour and 40 minutes.

Ingredients

        20 brussels sprouts, cleaned
         4 slices bacon, cut in pieces
         2 tablespoons garlic paste
         8 ice cubes
         1 teaspoon chicken bouillon granules

Instructions

Heat a water bath to 185°.

Cook the bacon, over medium heat, until brown and crisp (reserve the fat). Remove the bacon and place on a paper towel lined plate. Refrigerate the bacon until ready to serve. Allow the bacon to come to room temperature before serving. Turn the heat up to medium high, and add the cleaned brussels sprouts to the skillet with the reserved fat from the bacon. Shaking the skillet, lightly brown the brussels sprouts on all sides. Remove and cool.

In a bag, add the garlic paste on one side of the bag. Add the cooled brussels sprouts, placing them on top of the garlic paste. Sprinkle the chicken bouillon granules on top. Add the ice cubes. Remove the air and seal the bag. Place in the water bath for 90 mins. Plate and top with reserved bacon crumbles.

Recipe Notes

Carmelized onions are a wonderful addition to the brussels sprouts if so desired. Brown the sliced onions in a skillet until carmelized.   Allow the onions to cool. Add the onions to the brussels sprouts in the bag.

Butternut Squash Casserole

- Serves: 8.
- Preparation time is 5 minutes.
- Cooking time is 2 hours.

Ingredients

20	ounces butternut squash, peeled & chopped
4	tablespoons butter
2	tablespoons shallots, finely chopped
1 1/2	teaspoons garlic, minced
2	teaspoons grapeseed oil
1	teaspoon salt
6	ounces mushrooms thinly sliced
1	cup quinoa, rinsed
2	cups beef broth
1	cup Gruyere, shredded

Instructions

Heat a water bath to 185 °.

Place the diced butternut squash and butter in a bag. Remove the air and seal. Place the bag in the water bath and cook for 2 hours.

Saute the mushrooms in a large sauce pan, over medium high heat, in the grapeseed oil. Cook until they have browned. Lower the heat to medium low and add the shallots and the minced garlic. Cook until translucent. *Add the rinsed quinoa, salt and beef broth. Bring to a boil and reduce to a low simmer. Cover. Cook for about ten minutes until all of the broth has been absorbed. Remove the squash from the water bath and fold into the cooked quinoa. Stir in the grated gruyere cheese. Mix well until everything is incorporated. Serve.

If you wish to serve the Butternut casserole at a later time, put the casserole into a bag or in individual ramekins. Remove the air and seal and place back into the water bath to hold. If you wish to serve at a later time, allow the casserole to cool and refrigerate.

Recipe Notes

*Make sure that you rinse the quinoa until the water runs clear through a fine mesh strainer. To neglect this step will result in an unpleasant bitter taste.

You may substitute chicken or vegetable stock for the beef stock. They are all equally delicious.

Cabbage

- Serves: 4.
- Preparation time is 10 minutes.
- Cooking time is 1 1/2 hours.

Ingredients

1 head cabbage, sliced
5 tablespoons margarine
2 tablespoons caraway seeds

Instructions

Heat a water bath to 185°.

Remove the core from the cabbage and the outer leaves. Slice and place in a bag. Place the margarine on top. Remove the air and seal the bag. Place in the water bath for 90 minutes.

Toast the caraway seeds in a small skillet. Be careful not to burn them. Serve the cabbage and top with the caraway seeds.

Recipe Notes

This is a perfect side dish for the brisket recipe.

Cheddar Broccoli & Rice Casserole

- Serves: 6.
- Preparation time is 10 minutes.
- Inactive preparation time is 10 minutes.
- Cooking time is 2 hours.

Ingredients

        12 ounces mushrooms thinly sliced
         1 small onion, chopped
         2 ounces low fat cream cheese
       1/2 cup Gruyere, shredded
       1/2 cup Swiss cheese, shredded
         1 cup cheddar cheese, shredded
       1/4 cup Imagine mushroom soup
       1/4 cup chicken stock
         2 cups brown rice in a bag, prepared
         1 head broccoli
         2 tablespoons mayonnaise
         1 9 x 5 metal loaf pan

Instructions

Heat a water bath to 185°.

Cut up the broccoli into flowerettes. Place the soup, chicken stock, and low fat cream cheese in a blender or food processor. Process until smooth. Add all of the cheese and process again until smooth. Place all of the ingredients into a loaf pan and mix well. Place the loaf pan in a large bag and pulse to seal. Cook for a minimum of two hours. Serve.

Dressing/Stuffing

- Serves: 6.
- Preparation time is 20 minutes.
- Cooking time is 45 minutes.

Ingredients

       6 cups bread, dried & cubed
       1 small onion, chopped
 1 1/2 stalks celery, finely chopped
       1 tablespoon garlic powder
 1 1/2 tablespoons dried sage
    1/2 tablespoon dried thyme
    1/4 cup chicken stock, to moisten bread
       2 tablespoons margarine, for sauteing
       1 teaspoon chicken bouillon granules

Instructions

Heat a water bath to 170°.

Melt the margarine in a skillet and add the onions and celery. Cook
until softened. Remove from heat.

Preheat an oven to 200°.

Place the bread onto a baking sheet. Sprinkle the spices on top of the
bread cubes. Place in the oven and bake for 20 to 30 minutes until
dried. Remove from oven and allow to cool. Sprinkle one teaspoon of
the chicken bouillon on top of the bread cubes. Place the cooled
bread into a bag and add the cooled vegetables. Mix until well
combined. Add enough chicken stock to soften the bread (about 1/4
cup). Mix well. Pulse to seal the bag and place in the water bath for
1/2 hour or until ready to serve.

Espuma Wasabi Potatoes

- Serves: 6.
- Preparation time is 15 minutes.
- Cooking time is 2 hours.

Ingredients

    1 medium yukon gold potato, peeled & cubed
    1 tablespoon butter
    1 tablespoon wasabi paste
    6 ounces heavy cream
1/4 cup chicken stock
    1 bunch fresh chives
    1 quart whipper

Instructions

Heat a water bath to 185°.

Place the cubed potatoes in a bag with the butter. Remove the air and seal. Cook for two hours.

Heat the cream and chicken broth in a sauce pan over low heat. Keep warm.

Place the cooked potatoes in the food processor. Squeeze in the wasabi paste. Process the potatoes and slowly add in the warm chicken stock/cream mixture. Process until completely pureed. Mixture should be thin enough that it will pass through a strainer/sieve easily.

Put hot water into the* whipper to warm the container. Pour the water out before you pour in the potato mixture. Pour the hot potatoes through a sieve/strainer into a whipper. Follow directions for the whipper. Serve immediately by putting into a glass or coffee mug, etc. and garnish with the snipped chives.

Recipe Notes

The potatoes may be held by placing the whipper into a 165° water bath until ready to serve. The water level will be half way up the whipper not submerged.

*A whipper is a container which uses N20 charges which will foam the contents within the container. For example heavy cream becomes whipped cream.

If you do not wish to use a whipper, make the potatoes as you would normally.

Tip: If the potatoes seem to thick, directly pour in additional hot cream/stock into the whipper container. Using a wooden spoon handle stir the liquid into the potatoes.

Fennel & Onion a la Parmesan

- Serves: 4.
- Preparation time is 10 minutes.
- Cooking time is 2 hours.

<u>Ingredients</u>

        1   medium onion, thinly sliced
        1   medium fennel bulb, thinly sliced
        4   tablespoons margarine
      1/2   cup Parmesan cheese, grated

<u>Instructions</u>

Heat a water bath to 185°.

Place fennel, onion and margarine in a bag. Remove the air and seal.
Place in the water bath and cook for 2 hours. Remove from bag and
plate. Sprinkle with Parmesan.

Fingerling potatoes

- Serves: 4.
- Preparation time is 5 minutes.
- Cooking time is 2 hours and 10 minutes.

Ingredients

    18 fingerling potatoes, sliced lengthwise
      4 slices bacon, cut in pieces
      2 tablespoons duck fat

Instructions

Heat a water bath to 185°.

Cook the bacon over medium heat until brown and crisp. Remove the bacon and drain on a paper towel lined plate. Turn the heat up to medium high and add the potatoes sliced side down to the bacon fat remaining in the skillet. Cook until lightly browned and flip over to the skin side. After skin has lightly browned remove the potatoes to a plate and let cool.

Place the duck fat in a bag. Add the potatoes and coat well. Remove the air and seal the bag. Cook for 2 hours. Remove from the bag and plate. Garnish with the reserved bacon.

Goat Cheese Cheesecake with Beets

- Serves: 4.
- Preparation time is 15 minutes.
- Cooking time is 4 hours.

Ingredients

8	ounces low fat cream cheese
8	ounces goat cheese
1	tablespoon sour cream
3	eggs
3	cups beets, peeled & diced into 1/2" cubes
1/2	cup water
1/4	cup red wine vinegar
4	tablespoons sugar in the raw
4	tablespoons margarine
4	14 ounce ramekins
1/2	cup pistachio nuts

Instructions

Place the vinegar, water and sugar in a bag that you will be cooking the beets in. Seal the bag without trying to remove the air and place in the freezer. Allow the mixture to freeze. This can be done overnight.

Heat a water bath to 185°.

Prepare the beets and place them into the frozen vinegar mixture. Remove the air and seal. Place in the water bath for 2 hours. After 2 hours, lower the water bath to 165°. Keep the beets in the water bath.

In a food processor, combine the cream cheese, goat cheese, and sour cream. Process until well incorporated. Add the eggs one at a time to the cheese mixture and process until incorporated. Pour the mixture equally among the ramekins. Place each ramekin in an individual bag and pulse to seal. Place in the water bath and cook for 2 hours. Remove the ramekins from the bath. Top each ramekin with the beets and garnish with the pistachio nuts.

Recipe Notes

Save the juice from the beets and any leftover beets to make a delicious borscht.

Goody Gouda Polenta

- Serves: 4.
- Preparation time is 5 minutes.
- Cooking time is 2 hours.

Ingredients

    3/4 cup instant polenta
      4 cups beef stock
      8 ounces gouda cheese, shredded
      4 tablespoons butter
      1 9"x5"glass loaf pan

Instructions

Heat a water bath to 183°.

Place 4 cups beef stock in a loaf pan with the 3/4 cup polenta. Place the loaf pan in a bag. Pulse to seal. Do not be concerned if a small amount of liquid overflows into the bag. Place in a water bath and cook for 2 hours.

Spoon into bowls and top each bowl with 1 tbls. butter and 1/4 shredded cheese. Mix into the hot polenta. Serve.

Green Chile Mac & Cheese

- Serves: 4.
- Preparation time is 10 minutes.
- Cooking time is 30 minutes.

Ingredients

    1/4 cup chicken stock
      6 ounces low fat cream cheese
      4 cups 4 cheese blend Mexican cheese
      4 ounces green chilies, chopped
      6 ounces elbow macaroni, prepared
      4 16 ounce ramekins

Instructions

Heat a water bath to 150°.

Cook pasta according to package directions. Drain and allow to cool and dry.

Equally divide the pasta into the ramekins. In a blender, combine the chicken stock, cream cheese and Mexican blend cheese. Process until smooth and pour into the pasta. The sauce should be thick not runny. If the sauce is too thin it will absorb into the pasta. Add the green chilies and mix well. Place each ramekin in an individual bag and pulse to seal. Place in water bath and cook for a 1/2 an hour. Remove from bags and serve.

Gruyere Scalloped Potatoes with Champagne Sauce

- Serves: 4.
- Preparation time is 10 minutes.
- Cooking time is 2 hours.

Ingredients

2	medium yukon gold potatoes, thinly sliced
2	large leeks, thinly sliced
16	ounces Gruyere, sliced
4	4 inch spring form pans
4	tablespoons butter, cut into small pieces
	Sauce
1	cup chicken stock
1/2	cup Champagne
1/2	teaspoon xanthan gum, for thickening
3/4	cup Parmesan cheese, grated

Instructions

Heat a water bath to 185°.

Clean the leeks and slice them very thin. Slice the cheese. Slice the potatoes as thin as possible. The thinner the slices the better.

Place a piece of cheese in the bottom of each 4 inch diameter spring form pan begin. Make sure the bottom of the pan is completely covered. The bottom of this dish will actually become the top of the dish when served. Next, layer some of the leeks and top with a layer of potato slices. Dot with some of the butter pieces. Layer with more cheese. Push down on the layers to compact. Repeat the layers one more time ending with the cheese on top. Place each pan in an individual 8 inch wide bag and pulse to seal. Place in water bath. Use a plate to keep the pans submerged in the water. Cook for two hours.

To make the sauce, heat the champagne in a sauce pan. Bring to a boil and reduce to a simmer. Simmer for two minutes. Add the chicken stock. Simmer over medium heat for about 5 minutes. Add the xanthan gum and allow to thicken, stirring constantly. Lower the heat to low and stir in the* parmesan cheese. Keep stirring untill the cheese has melted completely.

Remove the pans from their bags and place them upside down on individual warmed plates. Release the spring and gently remove the pan. Using a knife remove the bottom of the pan which will now be on the top of the potatoes. Pour the sauce over the top and serve.

Recipe Notes

WARNING THIS RECIPE CONTAINS ALCOHOL.

*Use a very good block of Parmesan cheese and grate it yourself. Processed Parmesan tends to not melt well.

Kicked up Corn on the Cob

- Serves: 4.
- Preparation time is 10 minutes.
- Cooking time is 2 hours.

Ingredients

     8 corn on cob
     2 tablespoons chili powder
     2 tablespoons cumin
   10 tablespoons margarine
     4 tablespoons lime zest

Instructions

Heat a water bath to 185°.

Shuck the corn and remove the silk. Sprinkle chili powder and cumin evenly over the ears. Divide corn into two portions (2 bags). Sprinkle lime zest on top of corn.   * Put 5 tbls. of margarine in each bag. Remove the air and seal. Cook for 2 hours.

Recipe Notes

* You may use butter spray instead of the margarine. The spray will coat the corn and the spices will adhere well.

Lemon Potatoes

- Serves: 4.
- Preparation time is 10 minutes.
- Inactive preparation time is 10 minutes.
- Cooking time is 2 hours.

Ingredients

6 medium yukon gold potatoes, cut into 1/2" cubes
1/4 cup lemon juice
1/2 cup chicken stock
1 tablespoon basil
1 teaspoon salt
6 tablespoons margarine

Instructions

Place the chicken stock and the lemon juice in a bag which is large enough to later contain the potatoes. It is not necessary to remove all of the air but seal the bag. Place the bag in the freezer and allow the liquid to freeze. This can be done the night before.

Heat a water bath to 185°.

Remove the bag from the freezer. Season the cubed potatoes with the basil and salt. Place the potatoes in the bag. Top the potatoes with the margarine. Pulse to seal the bags and place in the water bath for two hours. Remove from bath and serve.

Recipe Notes

Save any of the leftover potatoes for lemon tarragon potato salad.

Lemon Tarragon Potato Salad

- Serves: 8.
- Preparation time is 10 minutes.
- Cooking time is 2 hours.

<u>Ingredients</u>

    6 medium yukon gold potatoes, sliced 1" thick
    1 small onion, chopped
    2 bunches scallions, chopped
    4 hardboiled eggs, sliced
    4 pieces bacon, cooked & chopped
  1/2 cup dijon mustard
  1/2 cup mayonnaise
1 1/2 tablespoons tarragon

<u>Instructions</u>

To make the potatoes see the recipe for Lemon potatoes. Cook and allow to cool.

In a large mixing bowl, add the dijon mustard and mayonnaise. Stir to combine. Add the tarragon and stir well. Add the remaining ingredients. Chill.

Mexican Rice

- Serves: 2.
- Preparation time is 10 minutes.
- Cooking time is 15 minutes.

Ingredients

1	package brown rice in a bag
14	ounces chunky tomato soup
14	ounces pinto beans, drained & rinsed
1	tablespoon cumin
1	tablespoon chili powder
1	bunch scallions, thinly sliced
1	cup cheddar cheese, shredded

Instructions

Remove the rice from the bag and place in a sauce pan. *Cook according to package directions but substitute the tomato soup for the water. Add the spices and the beans to the rice while cooking. Garnish with the scallions and cheddar cheese.

Recipe Notes

*Use this recipe as a base for the South of the Border Shrimp and Sausage soup.

Success Brown Rice in a Bag was used in this recipe.

Orange Liqueur Cranberries

- Serves: 4.
- Preparation time is 2 minutes.
- Cooking time is 1 hour.

Ingredients

    1 1/4 pounds frozen cranberries
    2/3 cup sugar in the raw
    12 ice cubes
    1 teaspoon orange liqueur

Instructions

Heat a water bath to 185°.

Place all ingredients in a bag. Remove the air and seal. Place in the water bath for 1 hour. Remove from the water bath and place in an ice bath for 1/2 an hour. Refrigerate until ready to serve.

Recipe Notes

WARNING THIS RECIPE CONTAINS ALCOHOL.

Parmesan Truffle Fries

- Serves: 2.
- Preparation time is 10 minutes.
- Cooking time is 15 minutes.

Ingredients

3 medium yukon gold potatoes, peeled and cut into strips
butter flavored cooking spray
1/2 cup Parmesan cheese, grated
2 tablespoons truffle oil

Instructions

Preheat oven to 485°.

Peel and slice potatoes into 1/4 inch thin strips. Place potato strips on an aluminum foil lined baking sheet that has been sprayed with butter flavored cooking spray. Place potatoes in a single layer evenly across sheet, making sure they are all making contact with the foil. Spray the tops of the potatoes with cooking spray. Place baking sheet on the bottom rack of the oven. Cook for approximately 8 mins. and remove from oven. Turn potatoes over to the other side. Cook until golden brown. Remove from the oven and drizzle with the truffle oil followed by the grated Parmesan. Serve.

Recipe Notes

This recipe was included (even though it is not sous vide) because it is such a great accompaniment to many of the sous vide recipes.

Red Bliss Potatoes w/onions

- Serves: 4.
- Preparation time is 5 minutes.
- Cooking time is 2 hours.

Ingredients

        16   red bliss potatoes, sliced in half
         2   medium onions, sliced
         7   tablespoons margarine
    1 1/2   tablespoons Old Bay seasoning

Instructions

Heat a water bath to 185°.

Place the onions and potatoes in a bag. Coat the vegetables with the Old Bay. Add the margarine. Remove the air and seal. Cook for 2 hours.

Rutabaga Souffle

- Serves: 4.
- Preparation time is 10 minutes.
- Inactive preparation time is 10 minutes.
- Cooking time is 2 1/2 hours.

Ingredients

    1 large rutabaga, cut into 1" cubes
       butter flavored cooking spray
    1 teaspoon thyme
    1 tablespoon kosher salt
    4 ounces low fat cream cheese
    6 egg yolks
    1 teaspoon sugar in the raw
 1/2 cup chicken stock
 1/2 cup Parmesan cheese, grated
    4 14 ounce ramekins

Instructions

Preheat an oven to 425°.

Place cut up rutabaga on a baking sheet that has been sprayed well with butter flavored cooking spray. Spray the rutabaga with the butter spray making sure to coat well on all sides. Sprinkle with the kosher salt and thyme. Roast in the oven for 20 minutes. Remove from the oven. Turn rutabaga over to the other side so that all sides will be browned. At this time, lower the oven temperature to 400 °. Roast for another 10 minutes. Remove from oven and allow to cool.

Heat a water bath to 165°.

In a food processor, combine the cooled rutabaga with one packet sugar in the raw and 1/4 cup of the chicken stock. Puree until smooth. Add the cream cheese and the remaining chicken stock. Process until smooth. Add the six egg yolks and process until well incorporated. Pour the mixture evenly into ramekins. Place each ramekin in an individual bag and pulse to seal. Cook in water bath for two hours.

Preheat a broiler. Remove ramekins from bags and sprinkle with parmesan cheese. Place under the broiler to melt the cheese or use a kitchen torch.

Recipe Notes

The rutabaga was not cooked by the sous vide method as it has a rather bitter acid flavor when cooked sous vide.

Savoury Mushroom Strata

- Serves: 8.
- Preparation time is 20 minutes.
- Cooking time is 2 hours.

Ingredients

    1 small onion, thinly sliced
    1 tablespoon garlic powder
  16 ounces wild mushrooms
    1 light beer
    1 tablespoon grapeseed oil, for sauteing
    2 cups heavy cream
1 1/2 teaspoons Worcestershire sauce
    1 teaspoon thyme
    1 cup gouda cheese, grated
    1 cup cheddar cheese, grated
    3 cups bread, dried
    4 large eggs
 1/4 cup molasses
    3 tablespoons spice mixture

Spice Mixture

    2 tablespoons kosher salt
2 1/2 tablespoons paprika
    2 tablespoons garlic powder
 1/4 teaspoon pepper
    1 tablespoon onion powder
    1 tablespoon cayenne pepper
    1 tablespoon oregano
    1 tablespoon thyme
    4 4 inch spring form pans

Instructions

Heat a water bath to 165°.

Saute the mushrooms with the garlic powder in grape seed oil, over high heat, until they are golden in color and reduced in size. Lower the heat to medium, and add the onions and cook until they are translucent and lightly browned. Add the beer and simmer until all of the liquid has evaporated. Remove from the heat and cool.

Cut the bread into 1/4 inch cubes. The bread should be stale, if not, dry it out in a 250° oven for 20 to 30 minutes. Place the bread in a large mixing bowl. In a separate mixing bowl, add the eggs and whisk. Add the molasses, cream, thyme, Worcestershire, and 3 tbls. spice mixture (kosher salt, paprika, garlic powder, pepper, onion powder, cayenne pepper, oregano, and thyme). Mix well and pour over bread cubes. Add the mushroom mixture and the grated cheese. Mix well until all ingredients are incorporated.

Equally divide the bread mixture into the spring form pans making sure the mixture is packed down. Place each pan in an individual 8 inch wide bag and pulse until the bag is secured tightly around the pan. Seal and cook for two hours.

Recipe Notes

This dish may be served as a main course which will serve four people or divide each spring form pan into two servings each for a side dish which will serve 8 people.

The extra spice mixture is great on chicken, meat and fish.

Spicy Green Beans

- Serves: 4.
- Preparation time is 5 minutes.
- Cooking time is 45 minutes.

Ingredients

    1 pound green beans, trimmed
    4 tablespoons butter
    2 tablespoons chicken flavored broth powder
    1 can Rotel diced tomatoes w/green chiles, drained

Instructions

Heat a water bath to 185°.

Clean the green beans. Add the beans to a bag. Add the chicken broth powder to the beans and shake to coat well. Add the butter and the drained Rotel tomatoes to the bag. Remove the air and seal. Place in water bath and submerge with a plate. Cook for 45 minutes. Remove from the water bath and plate.

Tomato Condift

- Serves: 4.
- Preparation time is 5 minutes.
- Inactive preparation time is 5 minutes.
- Cooking time is 2 hours.

<u>Ingredients</u>

  7 medium tomatoes
  3 tablespoons olive oil
  1 tablespoon oregano
  1 tablespoon basil

<u>Instructions</u>

Place the olive oil in a bag and seal. Place in the freezer and allow to harden.

Preheat a bath to 140°.

Wash and dry the tomatoes. Place them in the bag with the frozen olive oil. Add the herbs. Pulse to seal the bag. Place in the water bath and cook for 2 hours. Remove the tomatoes from the bag and pour into a bowl. Allow to cool to room temperature and serve.

Vegetable Medeley Casserole

- Serves: 4.
- Preparation time is 10 minutes.
- Cooking time is 2 1/2 hours.

Ingredients

    1/2 head cauliflower
    16 ounces frozen spinach, defrosted
    6 medium tomatoes, quartered
    1 large leek, sliced thin
    8 ounces Asiago cheese, sliced
    4 16 ounce ramekins
    1/2 cup white garlic marinade

Instructions

Heat a water bath to 185°.

Cut the cauliflower flowerettes into bite size pieces. Drain the defrosted spinach and squeeze out all of the liquid. Dry on a paper towel. Clean the leeks and thinly slice the white part only. Clean the tomatoes and cut into quarters. Slice the block of Asiago cheese into 1/4 inch thick slices.

Equally divide all of the vegetables and place in ramekins. Divide the marinade equally among the ramekins and stir well to coat the vegetables. Place the cheese slices on top. Place each ramekin in an individual bag and pulse to seal. Place in the water bath and cook for 2 1/2 hours. Serve.

Recipe Notes

Chateau Brand White Garlic Marinade was used in this recipe.

Zucchini Towers

- Serves: 4.
- Preparation time is 10 minutes.
- Cooking time is 1 1/2 hours.

<u>Ingredients</u>

  4 large zucchini, cut in thirds, crosswise
  6 ounces wild mushrooms, finely chopped
  1 medium onion, finely chopped
  1 tablespoon olive oil, for sauteing
  4 tablespoons tomato paste
1/2 cup Parmesan cheese, grated
  2 tablespoons basil
  2 tablespoons oregano
40 pieces pepperoni, chopped
  1 tablespoon garlic powder
12 teaspoons margarine

<u>Instructions</u>

Heat a water bath to 170°.

To make the zucchini fancier in appearance, score the sides of each zucchini with a zester or potato peeler. Be careful not to go to deeply into the zucchini. This makes stripes of white (the flesh) and green (the skin). Cut off the ends of each zucchini and divide into three equal pieces. Using a small melon baller carefully scoop out the inside of the zucchini. Leave about a 1/4 inch wall and do not go all the way to the bottom of the zucchini. Reserve the zucchini pulp for another recipe or make bread with it. Saute the onions and the garlic powder in the olive oil until translucent. Cool.

Put 1 tsp. margarine into each zucchini tower. Place the zucchini upright in a bag (three in each bag) and pulse to seal. Place in the water bath for 1 hour. Remove the zucchini from bags and cool. Lower the water bath to 150°.

In a mixing bowl, combine the sauteed onions, chopped mushrooms, pepperoni, tomato paste, basil, oregano and Parmesan cheese. Mix until well combined. Using a small spoon, spoon the mixture into each tower pressing down firmly. Place the zucchini (three in each) back into a bag and pulse to seal. Place back into the water bath. *Cook for 1/2 hour and serve.

Recipe Notes

* In order to keep the firmness of the towers, do not place back into the water bath until 1/2 hour before ready to serve. Do not cook for longer then 30 minutes.

Sauces

Bourguignon Sauce   204
Coney Sauce   206
Parmesan Sauce   207
Pimento Cheese Sauce   208
Red Wine Sauce   209

Bourguignon Sauce

- Serves: 4.
- Preparation time is 15 minutes.
- Cooking time is 1 hour and 15 minutes.

Ingredients

        2 celery stalks, chopped
        1 medium onion, chopped
        3 carrots, chopped
        5 garlic cloves, smashed
        1 tablespoon tomato paste
        2 tablespoons olive oil, for sauteing
        1 tablespoon thyme
        2 cups chicken stock
        4 cups beef broth
      1/2 cup dry red wine
        6 ounces wild mushrooms, thinly sliced
        1 tablespoon butter, for sauteing
        1 tablespoon veal demi glace
           cornstarch slurry

Instructions

Saute the onions, carrots, garlic and celery in olive oil over medium heat. Saute until soft. Mix in the tomato paste and cook for approximately one minute. Add the red wine and allow to almost completely cook down. Add the chicken stock and the beef broth. *Add the veal demi glaze and stir until dissolved into broth.   Bring to a boil and reduce to a simmer. Cover and simmer for approximately one hour. **Slowly add small amounts of the cornstarch slurry and stir until sauce has thickened.

Saute the mushrooms in the butter until they have browned. Strain sauce through a sieve. Discard vegetable mixture. Add the mushrooms to the strained sauce. Serve.

Recipe Notes

WARNING THIS RECIPE CONTAINS ALCOHOL.

*For the Lamb Bourguignon recipe you may substitute the veal demi-glaze for lamb demi-glaze.

**A cornstarch slurry is created by combining equal measures cornstarch dissolved into cold water. Add slowly to the sauce or you may over thicken and the sauce will become pasty tasting.

Coney Sauce

- Serves: 8.
- Preparation time is 5 minutes.
- Cooking time is 50 minutes.

Ingredients

     1   tablespoon butter
     2   medium onions, finely minced
   1/2   teaspoon garlic powder
   1/2   teaspoon salt
   1/2   teaspoon pepper
     2   tablespoons chili powder
 1 1/2   pounds ground round
     6   ounces tomato sauce
     6   ounces water
     1   tablespoon prepared yellow mustard
     1   teaspoon dry mustard
     5   hot dogs, finely ground

Instructions

In a large skillet, combine all of the ingredients except the hot dogs. Do not brown the beef or onions. Place everything in the skillet raw. Simmer the sauce for 30 mins.

Grind up the hot dogs in a food processor. Add the hot dogs to the meat mixture in the skillet and cook for another 20 mins. Put sauce on top of hot dogs, or use in the coney dog casserole.

Recipe Notes

You may also add beans to this and top hamburgers for a southwestern burger, or put on top of corn chips with cheese and make nachos.

Parmesan Sauce

- Serves: 2.
- Preparation time is 5 minutes.

Ingredients

     5 ounces Parmesan cheese, grated
     4 ounces low fat cream cheese
 1/3 cup chicken stock

Instructions

Grate the Parmesan cheese in a food processor. Add the cream cheese. While the processor is on, slowly add in the chicken stock. The mixture should not be thin. It should resemble the consistency of pancake batter.

Recipe Notes

For lemon Parmesan sauce add one tablespoon fresh lemon juice.

For tomato flavored sauce add two tablespoons tomato paste.

For pesto add two tablespoons pesto sauce.

Pimento Cheese Sauce

- Serves: 4.
- Preparation time is 5 minutes.

Ingredients

    3 ounces low fat cream cheese
    2 cups extra sharp cheddar cheese, shredded
    1/2 cup mayonnaise
    3 tablespoons pimientos, drained
    1/2 teaspoon garlic powder

Instructions

Combine all ingredients in a mixing bowl. Using an electric mixer, cream all ingredients. Keep in the refrigerator until ready to serve. Allow the sauce to come to room temperature before ready to serve. Serve as a sauce or a dip.

Recipe Notes

This sauce is used in the Chicken Meatball recipe.

Red Wine Sauce

- Serves: 2.
- Preparation time is 5 minutes.
- Cooking time is 15 minutes.

<u>Ingredients</u>

      2 shallots, finely chopped
      1 tablespoon garlic powder
      1 cup red wine
1 1/2 tablespoons margarine
      2 ounces veal demi glace

<u>Instructions</u>

Saute the shallots and garlic powder in margarine over medium heat. Cook until shallots are softened and translucent. Add the wine and reduce down until wine is about a 1/2 cup. Reduce heat to low and add the demi glace. Cook until demi glace has melted and is well incorporated into the wine. Remove from heat and serve or cool and store for future use.

<u>Recipe Notes</u>

WARNING THIS RECIPE CONTAINS ALCOHOL.

To use with meats in a sous vide process, pour sauce into a bag. Use a large bag as you may want to use this sauce with a roast. By making the bag larger it will allow you to place the roast in the bag. Seal but do no remove air. Place bag in the freezer and allow the sauce to become solid. Remove from the freezer and cut open bag. Remove the air and seal. Place back in freezer until needed.

You may wish to double or triple this recipe and place in two to three different bags and freeze for future use.

Pastry

Cornstarch Crepes   211
Gluten Free Savory Tomato & Onion Tart   213
Puff Pastry   215

Cornstarch Crepes

- Serves: 12.
- Preparation time is 5 minutes.
- Inactive preparation time is 5 minutes.
- Cooking time is 4 minutes.

<u>Ingredients</u>

    1 cup cornstarch
 1/8 teaspoon baking soda
    2 large eggs
    1 cup milk
 1/3 cup water
 1/4 teaspoon salt
    2 tablespoons butter, melted
       butter flavored cooking spray

<u>Instructions</u>

Place all of the ingredients (except cooking spray) in a food processor and process untill smooth. Refrigerate for 1 to 2 hours.

Heat a crepe pan over medium heat and spray with butter cooking spray. Ladle in the batter and swirl until it has completely covered the crepe pan. Pour out the excess batter. Wait until bubbles form and turn the crepe to the other side. Cook for about one minute. Place cooked crepes on a tea towel. Keep them warm or place them in a portion size bag after they have cooled.

The crepes will keep two days in the refrigerator and 2 months in the freezer. If you will be freezing the crepes, place wax paper between them. For freezer crepes remove them from the plastic bag and allow them to defrost. They should come apart easily when defrosted.

Recipe Notes

Fill the crepes with the Carmel Apple Walnut Topping (see recipe).

For more savory crepes, replace the 1/3 cup water with 1/3 cup chicken or beef broth.

For sun-dried tomato crepes, add 1/4 cup oil packed minced sun-dried tomatoes (patted dry) to batter.

For dessert crepes,-eliminate the salt. Add 2 tbls. sugar, 1 tsp. vanilla, and 1 tbls. cointreau, or amoretto, brandy or any other liqueur of choice.

For espresso crepes, add 2 tbls. fine powder espresso.

For chocolate crepes, replace 1 cup cornstarch with 3/4 cup cornstarch and 1/3 cup unsweetened cocoa powder. Replace 2 tbls. sugar with 1/4 cup sifted powdered sugar.

Gluten Free Savoury Tomato & Onion Tart

- Serves: 6.
- Preparation time is 10 minutes.
- Cooking time is 2 hours.

<u>Ingredients</u>

- 1 1/2 cups Pamela's Baking & Pancake Mix
- 4 tablespoons butter
- 2 tablespoons jalepeno lime oil
- 1/4 cup ice water
- 6 slices bacon, crumbled
- 1 large onion, sliced
- 4 tablespoons margarine
- 30 cherry tomatoes
- 2 tablespoons olive oil
- 1 tablespoon basil
- 1 tablespoon oregano
- 1 tablespoon garlic powder
- 1 avocado, sliced
- 1 tablespoon lime juice
- 6 slices Provolone cheese, slices
- 1/4 cup Parmesan cheese, grated

<u>Instructions</u>

Heat an oven to 350°.

Heat a water oven to 183°.

*For the crust
In a mixing bowl, combine the baking mix with the butter. Using a pastry knife cut the butter into the flour mixture until it is in very small pieces. Add the jalapeno lime oil. Slowly mix in the water. You may not need the whole amount. Mix until the dough comes together. You do not want it to be sticky. Using a 9 inch tart pan, press the dough into the pan using your fingers. Pierce the crust with a fork. * Cook in the oven until golden brown approximately 15 to 20 mins. Remove from oven and sprinkle the grated Parmesan on the crust. Cool.

Place the sliced onions in a bag with the 4 tbls. butter. Remove the air and seal. Place in the water bath. Place the olive oil, oregano, basil, and garlic powder in a bag and mix well. Add the tomatoes and coat them with the olive oil herb mixture. Pulse to seal and place in the water bath. Cook both the onions and tomatoes for 2 hours.

Preheat a broiler. Position the rack to the second from the top.

Cook the bacon and crumble into small pieces. Drain the butter from the onions by cutting a small hole in the bag and allow the liquid to drain out of the bag. Place the drained onions on top of the crust followed by the tomatoes. Top with the round pre-sliced provolone cheese. Place under the broiler to melt the cheese. Slice the avocado and sprinkle with the lime juice. Top the tart with the avocado slices and crumbled bacon. If you so desire, splash with the jalapeno lime oil. Enjoy.

Recipe Notes

*Keep an eye on the crust since every oven may cook differently.

Puff Pastry

- Serves: 4.
- Preparation time is 80 minutes.
- Cooking time is 20 minutes.

Ingredients

    1   egg, to coat
    2   cups flour
2 1/2 sticks unsalted butter, cut into 1/4 inch cubes
 2/3 cup cold water
 3/4 teaspoon salt

Instructions

Cut the butter into cubes. Place the butter in a freezer for about 20 minutes. In a food processor, process the flour, salt and 1 stick of the butter by pulsing. Process until no visible pieces of butter remain. Remove from bowl and put into a mixing bowl. Add the remaining chilled butter to the bowl. Using a rubber spatula, fold the butter into the mixture. Pour all but two tbls. of water into the bowl. Fold the water into the flour. Keep folding until mixture is completely moistened. If the flour is still dry add one tbls. at a time to the mixture. Turn flour mixture out onto a piece of plastic wrap and shape into a circle. Completely seal. Place in the refrigerator for at least 1 hour.

Preheat oven to 375 °. Spread the dough out into a circle about 1/4 inch thick on a floured board. Cut into rounds using whatever bowl you will be using for pot pies, etc, as a guide. Place rounds on parchment paper lined baking sheet. Place in the refrigerator for 20 minutes.

Crack the egg in a bowl and whisk. Using a pastry brush coat the tops of the rounds. Bake in the oven for 20 to 30 minutes until tops are browned. Serve.

Desserts

Apple Betty   217
Banana Cake   219
Chocolate Cherry Semi-freddo   221
Creme Anglais   222
Dulce de Leche   223
Flourless Chocolate Kalhua Cake   224
Fruit Tart   226
Godiva Carmel Cheesecake with Chocolate Cookies   227
Gooey Cinnamon Brown Sugar Apples   229
Key Lime Pie   230
Luscious Lemon Blueberry Bread Pudding   231
Peanut Butter and Apple Custard   232
Poached Pears with Cranberries and Stilton Cheese   234
Pumpkin Souffle   235
Rice Pudding   236
Vanilla Cherry Pudding   237
White Chocolate Chambord Pudding Cake   238

Apple Betty

- Serves: 4.
- Preparation time is 15 minutes.
- Cooking time is 4 hours and 45 minutes.

<u>Ingredients</u>

```
    1  cup applesauce
  1/4  cup brown sugar
    1  teaspoon vanilla extract
    1  teaspoon cinnamon
    1  teaspoon apple pie spice
    4  eggs
  1/4  cup sugar
    8  tablespoons margarine, melted
    4  14 ounce ramekins
       Sauce
    1  granny smith apple, cubed
  1/2  cup dulce de leche ( see recipe )
```

<u>Instructions</u>

Heat a water bath to 185°.

Peel and core the apples. Cut the apples into cubes. Place the cubed apples into a bag and spoon in the dulce de leche sauce. Pulse to seal. Place the bag in the water bath and cook for 45 minutes. Remove from bath and rapid chill the apples in an ice bath for 1/2 hour. Remove from the ice bath and refrigerate until ready to use.

Lower the water bath to 175 °.

Melt the butter in a microwave and cool. In a large mixing bowl, add the apple sauce, cinnamon, brown sugar, vanilla, and melted butter.

In a mixing bowl, using a stand mixer, add the 4 eggs and the 1/4 cup sugar. Whisk on high for 5 to 8 minutes until the eggs have doubled in size and have become light and fluffy.

Fold 1/3 of eggs into applesauce mixture. Repeat two more times until all of the eggs are incorporated. Pour the batter, equally, into each ramekin. Put each ramekin into an individual bag and pulse to seal.

Place in the water bath and cook for 4 hours. Remove from water bath and place ramekins (still in their bags) in an ice bath for 1/2 hour. Remove from the ice bath and refrigerate until 1/2 hour before ready to serve. Top the ramekins with the cubed apples in dulce de leche sauce. Serve.

Banana Cake

- Serves: 6.
- Preparation time is 15 minutes.
- Inactive preparation time is 15 minutes.
- Cooking time is 6 hours.

<u>Ingredients</u>

          3 cups fresh bread crumbs
       3/4 cup dark brown sugar
          4 bananas
     1 1/2 teaspoons cinnamon
       1/4 teaspoon nutmeg
          1 teaspoon allspice
       1/2 cup walnuts, chopped
       1/2 cup dulce de leche, see recipe
          3 eggs
          1 cup container of whipped cream topping, for garnish
          1 6" spring form pan

<u>Instructions</u>

Preheat an oven to 200°.

Mix the bread crumbs with the spices and the walnuts. Place on a baking sheet and bake in the oven for approximately 20 to 30 minutes until the bread is toasted.

Heat a water bath to 165°.

In a food processor, puree the bananas and the brown sugar until smooth. Pour into a large mixing bowl and add the dried bread crumb mixture to the bananas. Stir until well incorporated.

In a separate mixing bowl, using a stand mixer with a whisk attachment, add the eggs and process on high until eggs become frothy and double in size. This should take 5 to 10 minutes.

Add 1/3 of the egg mixture to the banana mixture and gently fold in until the egg is completely incorporated. Repeat this process two more times.

Pour mixture into a six inch spring form pan. Place in a bag and pulse to seal allowing gentle pressure of the bag to touch the top of the mixture. If some of the mixture overflows, do not worry as you will be removing the sides of the pan along with the overflowed cooked mixture. Place in water bath and cook for 6 hours. Make sure to submerge with plates as the bag will become buoyant. In a separate bag, spoon in the dulce de leche sauce. Pulse to seal. Place in the water bath a 1/2 hour before ready to serve. Remove the banana cake from bag and allow to cool. Release the spring on the pan and remove. Remove the dulce de leche sauce from bath. Snip off one corner of the bag and squeeze the sauce out on top of the banana cake. Top with the whipped cream. Serve.

Chocolate Cherry Semi-freddo

- Serves: 8.
- Cooking time is 1 hour and 15 minutes.

Ingredients

12	ounces chocolate chips
1/4	cup heavy cream
6	egg whites, separate out yolks
1 1/3	cups heavy cream
2	cups cherries, stems and pitts removed
1/2	cup extra fine sugar

Instructions

Place the *eggs in a cold water bath. Heat the bath to 135°. When the temperature of the water bath has stabilized at 135°, cook the eggs for 1 hour and 15 minutes. Remove the eggs from the bath and store in the refrigerator. This pasturizes the eggs. The eggs must be cold for this recipe.

In a bain marie, heat the chocolate and the 1/4 cup cream. Keep stirring until mixture is melted and smooth. Remove from heat and allow to cool.

Separate the egg yolks from the whites, reserving the whites. Stir the yolks into the cooled chocolate mixture. In a mixing bowl, beat the egg whites until fluffy. In another mixing bowl, whip the cream and slowly add the sugar. Continue until soft peaks are formed.

Cut the cherries in half. Fold the egg whites into the chocolate mixture. Fold in the whipped cream. Add the cherries. Using a large loaf pan, line the pan with plastic wrap, allowing the sides to hang over the edges. Pour the mixture into the loaf pan. Completely seal the mixture with the plastic wrap. Place in the freezer overnight.

Recipe Notes

*The eggs are cooked in their shells and stored in their shells in the refrigerator. This process pasteurizes the eggs and may be used in recipes calling for raw eggs such as salad dressings, etc.

Creme Anglais

- Serves: 6.
- Preparation time is 5 minutes.
- Cooking time is 30 minutes.

Ingredients

     1 can sweetened condensed milk
     4 egg yolks
   1/2 cup heavy cream
     1 16 ounce ramekin

Instructions

Heat a water bath to 179°.

Mix all ingredients together and pour into a ramekin. Place the ramekin in a bag. Pulse to seal.

Place in the water bath and cook for 30 minutes. Take the bag out of the water bath and place in an ice bath for 1/2 an hour. Remove the bag from the ice bath. Using a hand blender, blend mixture until any lumps in the mixture disappear. You may also process in a food processor until smooth. Refrigerate until ready to use.

Recipe Notes

This sauce has a myriad of uses, such as, pouring over fresh fruit or as a base for rice pudding and tarts. You may also use this as a base for ice cream.

Dulce de leche

- Serves: 6.
- Preparation time is 2 minutes
- Cooking time is 24 hours.

Ingredients

     1 can sweetened condensed milk
     1 16 ounce ramekin

Instructions

Heat a water bath to 170°.

Place the sweetened condensed milk into a ramkein. Place ramekin in a bag and pulse to seal. The bag should be putting gentle pressure on the mixture. Place in the water bath and cook for 24 hours. Remove from bag and allow to cool. Refrigerate until ready to use.

Flourless Chocolate Kahlua Cake

- Serves: 2.
- Preparation time is 15 minutes.
- Inactive preparation time is 15 minutes.
- Cooking time is 3 hours.

<u>Ingredients</u>

1/4	pound unsalted butter, cut in cubes
1/2	pound semisweet chocolate, coarsely chopped
2	tablespoons Kahlua
4	large eggs
2	tablespoons sugar
1/2	teaspoon vanilla extract
1/4	teaspoon salt
1	cup fresh raspberries
5	6 ounce ramekins
1/2	cup container of whipped cream topping

<u>Instructions</u>

Heat a water bath to 175 °.

In a double boiler, combine the chocolate, butter, and Kahlua. Place the mixture over a medium saucepan of water that is boiling. Melt the mixture, stirring constantly until smooth and creamy (approximately 5 minutes). Set aside to cool down.

Meanwhile, using a stand mixer, combine the eggs, sugar, vanilla, and salt. Whisk until the mixture almost doubles in volume and becomes frothy. This should take about 5 to 10 minutes. Fold 1/3 of the egg mixture into the chocolate mixture using a rubber spatula. Gently fold the egg mixture into the chocolate until combined. Repeat this process two more times until all of the egg mixture is combined with the chocolate. Pour the mixture, equally, into the 6 ounce ramekins.

Place each ramekin in an individual bag and pulse until bag begins to press on top of the chocolate mixture. Seal and place in the water bath. Cook for 3 hours. Remove the ramekins from the water bath and submerge into an ice bath. Leave the ramekins in the ice bath for a 1/2 hour. You may now refrigerate or remove the ramekins from the bags. Top with fresh raspberries and whipped cream.

Recipe Notes

WARNING THIS RECIPE CONTAINS ALCOHOL WHICH HAS NOT BEEN COOKED OUT.

Fruit Tart

- Serves: 6.
- Preparation time is 20 minutes.
- Inactive preparation time is 20 minutes.

Ingredients

1 prepared graham cracker crust
1 jar apricot jam, for glazing
1 Creme Anglais, prepared
1 pint strawberries, halved
1 kiwifruit, sliced
1 pint blueberries
1 pint raspberry

Instructions

Make the Creme Anglais according to directions (see recipe). Cool and pour into prepared graham cracker crust. Refrigerate for at least two hours.

Make the glaze by placing the apricot jam in a sauce pan over low heat. When the jam has melted, remove from heat and allow it to cool to room temperature.

Take the tart out of the refrigerator and place a row of strawberries around the outer edge. Next follow with a row of sliced kiwi. Place the raspberries mounded up in the center. Place the blueberries in the spaces between the strawberries. With a pastry brush carefully apply the glaze over the fruit. Refrigerate for at least 30 minutes.

Godiva Carmel Cheesecake with Chocolate Cookies

- Serves: 6.
- Preparation time is 20 minutes.
- Cooking time is 3 hours.

Ingredients

16	ounces low fat cream cheese
8	Pamela's extreme chocolate mini cookies, crumbled
1	bag of Pamela's extreme chocolate mini cookies, for crust
3/4	cup extra fine sugar
2	tablespoons butterscotch carmel topping
2	eggs
2	tablespoons Godiva liqueur
3	4" dia. spring form pans

Instructions

Make the crust in the spring form pans according to the package directions. This is done in a regular oven. Allow to cool.

Heat a water bath to 165°.

In a mixing bowl, cream together the sugar and the cream cheese. Add the carmel sauce and the Godiva liqueur. Add the eggs one at a time and blend until all ingredients are well incorporated. Mix in by hand the crumbled chocolate cookies.

*Pour the cream cheese into the 4 inch diameter spring form pans with the prepared crust. Place each in an individual bag and pulse to seal. Do not over pulse or the liquid will be sucked out of the pan. Place in the water bath and weight down with plates. Cook for 3 hours.

Remove from the water bath and submerge in a ice water bath. Allow the cheesecakes to remain in the ice bath for 1 hour. Remove the cheesecakes from the bags and cover with plastic wrap. Place the cheesecakes in the refrigerator until ready to serve. Run a knife around the perimeter of the pan before releasing the spring. Remove the pan with the bottom remaining. Place on serving plates.

<u>Recipe Notes</u>

WARNING THIS RECIPE CONTAINS ALCOHOL WHICH HAS NOT
BEEN COOKED OUT.

*Pour the mixture into one spring form and immediately pulse to seal it.
Repeat the process with the remaining spring form pans. This
prevents the mixture from running out of the bottom of the pan. When
the bag is sealed tightly around the pan it stops the mixture from
escaping out of the bottom.

This recipe is gluten free.

Gooey Cinnamon Brown Sugar Apples

- Serves: 6.
- Preparation time is 20 minutes.
- Cooking time is 4 hours.

<u>Ingredients</u>

1	pound low fat cream cheese
1/2	cup extra fine sugar
3/4	cup brown sugar
4	tablespoons butter, melted
2 1/4	tablespoons cinnamon
3/4	tablespoon vanilla extract
6	granny smith apples, washed
2	eggs
6	16 ounce ramekins

<u>Instructions</u>

Preheat a water bath to 165°.

In a mixing bowl, using an electric beater, cream together the cream cheese, extra fine sugar and vanilla. Add the eggs to the mixture.

Melt the butter in a microwave oven. Combine the brown sugar and cinnamon together and stir into the melted butter.

Wash the apples. Cut off the top of the apples and reserve. Remove the air and seal the tops immediately in a bag to keep them from turning brown. Using a melon baller, scoop out the insides of the apple, removing the core. Keep a 1/4 inch thickness of the apple. Pour the cream cheese mixture into each prepared apple. Pour the melted butter/brown sugar mixture in each one and using a knife swirl into cheesecake mixture. Carefully place each apple in a ramekin and into an individual bag. Pulse to seal. Place in the water bath and weight down with a heavy plate. Cook for 4 hours. Two hours before serving add the reserved apple tops into the water bath. Cook for the remaining two hours. Remove from water bath and cool in an ice bath for 1 hour. Remove from ice bath and refrigerate to keep cool. To serve, place on a plate and top with the reserved top of the apple.

Key Lime Pie

- Serves: 6.
- Preparation time is 20 minutes.
- Inactive preparation time is 20 minutes.
- Cooking time is 2 hours.

Ingredients

1	package mini ginger cookies
3	tablespoons margarine
1	can sweetened condensed milk
4	egg yolks
1/2	cup key lime juice
6	4" dia. spring form pans
1	container of whipped cream topping
2	limes, sliced for garnish

Instructions

Preheat a water bath to 165°.

*Follow the directions on cookie package for crumb crust. Cook the crust in the spring form pans in a regular oven. Cool the crusts by placing in the refrigerator.

In a mixing bowl, combine the sweetened condensed milk and the key lime juice. In a separate bowl, whisk the egg yolks. Add the yolks to the mixing bowl with the other ingredients. Stir until well incorporated.

Pour custard mixture into the cooled spring form pans. Place each spring form pan in a separate bag and pulse to seal. Place in a water bath for 2 hours.

Remove from the water bath and place in an ice bath for one hour to cool and set the custard. Refrigerate until ready to serve. Top with whipped cream and lime slices.

Recipe Notes

*Pamela's mini ginger cookies were used for this recipe.

Luscious Lemon Blueberry Bread Pudding

- Serves: 6.
- Preparation time is 10 minutes.
- Cooking time is 3 hours.

Ingredients

  5 cups stale bread, cut into 1/4" cubes
  1 pint blueberries, frozen, defrosted
14 ounces sweetened condensed milk
  2 cups heavy cream
  1 teaspoon lemon extract
  1 teaspoon vanilla extract
  4 tablespoons brown sugar
  3 eggs
  1 9"x5"glass loaf pan
  1 container of whipped cream topping, for garnish

Instructions

Heat a water bath to 165°.

In a large mixing bowl, combine the sweetened condensed milk, cream, vanilla, brown sugar and lemon extract. In a separate bowl, whisk the eggs. Add the eggs to the cream mixture. Stir in the stale bread and the blueberries. Make sure everything is well combined.

Pour the mixture into the loaf pan. Place the pan in a large bag and pulse to seal. The bag should be putting light pressure on top of the mixture in the pan. Place in a water bath. Weight down with a plate. Cook for 3 hours. Remove from bag and scoop onto plates. Garnish with whipped cream.

Recipe Notes

If you do not have stale bread, use fresh bread. Heat a oven to 250°. Place the cubed bread on a baking sheet. Cook for approximately 1/2 an hour or until bread becomes dry.

Peanut Butter & Apple Custard

- Serves: 6.
- Preparation time is 15 minutes.
- Cooking time is 4 hours.

<u>Ingredients</u>

1/2 cup peanut butter
1 can sweetened condensed milk
8 ounces low fat cream cheese
5 egg yolks
1 1/2 tablespoons cinnamon
3 tablespoons brown sugar
3 tablespoons margarine
3 granny smith apples, cored & peeled
5 5 3/4 ounces flan ramekins

<u>Instructions</u>

Heat a water bath to 185°.

In a mixing bowl, combine the peanut butter, sweetened condensed milk, and the cream cheese. Using an electric mixer, mix until smooth. In a separate bowl, whisk the egg yolks. Add the egg yolks to the peanut butter mixture. Pour custard into the ramekins. Put each ramekin in an individual 8 inch wide bag (make sure the bag has plenty of length). Pulse to seal. Place in the refrigerator until ready to cook.

Peel and core the apples. Slice into 1/2 inch thick slices. Place in a bag. Add the cinnamon and brown sugar and coat the apple slices. Top with the margarine. Remove the air and seal. Place apples in the water bath and cook for 1 hour. Remove from the water bath and cool in an ice bath for 1 hour. Refrigerate.

Lower the water bath to 165°.

Place the custards in the water bath. Cook for 3 hours. Remove the custards from the bags. Keep the water bath at 165° for reheating the apples. * Let the custards cool and refrigerate for one hour before serving. Reheat the apples in the water bath one half hour before serving. Remove the warmed apples from the bath. Open the bag containing the apples and spread apples on top of custards. Spoon the sauce over the apples. Serve.

Recipe Notes

*If you will not be serving the custards on the day you have cooked them, you must place them (still within their bags) in an ice bath for one hour and refrigerate.

Reheat the apples before serving. If you wish to serve the apples cold, the sauce will have congealed. Remove the apples from the congealed sauce before serving.

Poached Pears with Cranberries and Stilton cheese

- Serves: 4.
- Preparation time is 15 minutes.
- Cooking time is 3 hours.

Ingredients

    2 pears, halved
1/2 cup dried cranberries
1/2 cup red wine
    1 tablespoon brown sugar
    1 tablespoon vanilla extract
2 1/2 ounces Stilton cheese
1/2 cup toasted walnuts
    4 16 ounce ramekins

Instructions

Heat a water bath to 167°.

Peel, halve and core the pears. Equally stuff the pears with the cranberries and half of the Stilton cheese (the other half will be used for garnishing). Place pears in an individual ramekin. In a bowl, combine the vanilla, brown sugar and the red wine. Pour the wine evenly on top of the pears. Place each ramekin in an individual bag. Pulse to seal just until the wine begins to come up and cover the pears. Cook for 3 hours.

Toast the walnuts in a skillet. Remove the pears from the bags and top with the remaining cheese and toasted walnuts.

Recipe Notes

WARNING THIS RECIPE CONTAINS ALCOHOL WHICH HAS NOT BEEN COOKED OUT.

This may also be made to top salad greens and served as a first course.

Pumpkin Souffle

- Serves: 4.
- Preparation time is 15 minutes.
- Cooking time is 3 hours.

<u>Ingredients</u>

       1 15 ounce pumpkin, canned
       2 sticks margarine, melted
       1 teaspoon ginger
     2/3 tablespoon cinnamon
     1/2 teaspoon nutmeg
     1/2 tablespoon cloves, ground
   1 1/2 cups sugar
       8 eggs, separate out yolks
       4 16 ounce ramekins
       1 container of whipped cream topping

<u>Instructions</u>

Heat a water bath to 175 °.

In a mixing bowl, separate 8 eggs yolks from the whites. Discard whites or save for another recipe. Whisk together the yolks (using a stand mixer) with the 1/4 cup of the sugar. Mix on high for 5 to 10 minutes.

In another mixing bowl, mix the remaining sugar with the pumpkin, melted margarine and spices. Fold in 1/3 of the egg mixture, completely incorporating into the pumpkin mixture. Repeat two more times until all of the eggs have been incorporated.

Pour mixture equally into ramekins. Place in individual bags and pulse until bag puts light pressure on top of pumpkin mixture. Seal and place in water bath. Cook for 3 hours. Remove from water bath and plate. Top with whipped cream.

Rice Pudding

- Serves: 6.
- Preparation time is 15 minutes.
- Inactive preparation time is 15 minutes.
- Cooking time is 1 hour.

Ingredients

       Creme Anglais (see recipe)
1/2 teaspoon ground cinnamon
2 cups brown rice in a bag
6 16 ounce ramekins
2 tablespoons dark rum
1/4 cup raisins

Instructions

Heat a water bath to 175°.

*Cook rice according to package directions. Allow rice to cool.

Make the Creme Anglais. In a large mixing bowl, combine the Creme Anglais, the ground cinnamon and the cooked rice. Pour the mixture equally into the ramekins. Place each ramekin in an individual bag and pulse to seal. Place in the water bath and cook for a minimum of one hour. Meanwhile, macerate the raisins in the dark rum for 1/2 an hour.

Remove the ramekins from bags. Stir the raisins into the ramekins. Serve.

Recipe Notes

*Success Brown rice in a bag was used for this recipe.

This recipe may also be served cold if so desired.

Vanilla Cherry Pudding

- Serves: 6.
- Preparation time is 10 minutes.
- Cooking time is 2 hours.

Ingredients

4	eggs
3/4	cup sugar
1 1/2	teaspoons vanilla extract
1/4	teaspoon salt
3	cups heavy cream
3	16 ounce ramekins
1	cup slivered almonds, toasted
28	ounces cherry pie filling
6	sprigs of mint, for garnish

Instructions

Heat a water bath to 165°.

In a mixing bowl, whisk the eggs. Add the sugar, vanilla, salt, and cream. Mix well. Pour mixture into ramekins. Place each ramekin in an individual bag and pulse to seal. Place in water bath and cook for 2 hours. Remove the ramekins from the water bath and place in an ice bath for 1 hour. Refrigerate until ready to serve.

To serve, layer the custard, cherries and toasted almonds in equal amounts into tall parfait glasses. Garnish with toasted almonds on top and a sprig of mint.

White Chocolate Chamboard Pudding Cake

- Serves: 3.
- Preparation time is 20 minutes.
- Cooking time is 4 hours.

Ingredients

    8 tablespoons butter, cubed
    8 ounces white chocolate baking bars, chopped
    2 tablespoons Chambord
    4 eggs
    1/2 teaspoon vanilla extract
    1/4 teaspoon salt
    3 16 ounce ramekins
    <u>Sauce</u>
    1 tablespoon sugar
    1 pint raspberries
    1/8 teaspoon xanthan gum
    container of whipped cream topping, for garnish

Instructions

Heat a water bath to 175°.

In a bain marie, melt the chocolate, butter and the Chamboard. Stir constantly until everything has completely melted. Remove from heat and let cool.

Combine the eggs, sugar, vanilla, and salt in a mixing bowl. Using a stand mixer, whisk for 6 to 10 minutes until mixture has doubled in size and has become light and frothy.

Fold 1/3 of the egg mixture into the cooled chocolate. Repeat this two more times until egg mixture is completely incorporated into the chocolate. Pour the mixture into the ramekins. Place each ramekin in an individual bag and pulse to seal. The bag should be putting light pressure on top of the mixture. Place in a water bath and cook for 3 hours. Remove the ramekins from the water bath and submerge in an ice bath to quickly chill down. Maintain the water bath at 175° for the sauce which will be cooked an hour before serving. * Leave in the ice water bath for 1/2 hour if you will be serving immediately, otherwise keep it in the ice water bath for an hour. Refrigerate until ready.

One hour before serving, place 1/2 the raspberries into a bag with 1 tbls. sugar to coat. Remove the air and seal the bag. Cook for one hour in the 175° water bath. Remove the berry mixture from the bag and pour into a bowl. Add the xanthan gum to the cooked berries. Whisk until thickened. Spoon sauce over cakes and top with fresh berries. Garnish with the whipped cream.

Recipe Notes

*The cakes can be served at room temperature or chilled.

A

Accompaniment
Coney Sauce,206
Parmesan Sauce,207
Pimento Cheese
Sauce,208
Red Wine Sauce,209

Anchovy paste
Greek Style Lamb
burgers,67

Andouille sausage
Chicken on Horseback,64
Jambalaya,148
South of the Border
Shrimp
and Sausage Soup,36
Spicy Black Bean Soup,37

Appetizer
Foie Gras Brulee,21
Garlic Escargot w/Kasseri
Cheese,23
Mexican Cheese &
Chicken Dip,26
Mussels in lemon Grass
Curry Coconut Broth, 27
Pimento Cheese
Sauce,208
Pineapple Mango Duck
Nachos,30
Pizzaola Hamburgers
Sliders,31
Polenta Crackers with
Sausage & Meatballs,32
Pork & Shrimp
Dumplings,34
Spinach Artichoke Dip,38
Vichyssoise,39

Apples,
Apple Betty,217
Carmel Apple Walnut
Topping for Pancakes,44
Gooey Cinnamon Brown
Sugar Apples,229
Peanut Butter Apple
Custard,232
Pork Loins with
Apple/Cranberry
Stuffing,99

Applesauce,
Apple Betty,217

Apricot,
Apricot Stuffed French
Toast,41
Fruit Tart,226

Artichokes,
Spinach Artichoke Dip, 38
Lemon Chicken,133

Asiago,
Italian Chicken Zucchini
Bundles,131
Spinach Artichoke Dip,38
Vegetable Medley
Casserole,200

Asparagus,
Asparagus,167
Fiesta Rice Egg Cups
w/Jumbo Lump Crab,46
Veal Scallopine with
Prosciutto and
Asparagus,115

Avocado,
    Bison Burgers,60
    Gluten Free Savoury
    Tomato & Onion Tart,213
    Sante Fe Pork Tacos,71

B

Baby Portabello mushrooms,
    Brandied Butter
    Mushrooms,170

Bacon,
    Brussels Sprouts,171
    Buffalo Chicken
Burgers,61
    Cheddar Potato Soup,18
    Chicken Meatballs
    w/Pimento Cheese
    Sauce,63
    Fingerling potatoes,180
    Gluten Free Savoury
    Tomato & Onion Tart,213
    Lemon Chicken,133
    Lemon Tarragon Potato
    Salad,189
    Parmesan Baskets
    w/Savoury Tomato Egg
    Cups,55
    Shrimp Caesar Pizza,161

Balsamic,
    Foie Gras Brulee,21

Bamboo Shoots,
    Chinese Chicken Lettuce
    Wraps,65

Banana,
    Banana Cake,219

Barbecue sauce
    Sloppy Joes,73

Basil,
    Chicken Margarita,118
    Chicken on Horseback,62
    Chicken Parmesan,119
    Chicken Prosciutto Pie,121
    Eggplant Lasagna,85
    Gluten Free Savoury
    Tomato & Onion Tart,213
    Halibut a la Parmesan,146
    Italian Chicken Zucchini
    Bundles,131
    Italian Frittata,51
    Italian Pizza Custard,89
    Italian Portabellos,91
    Lasagna Bolognese,94
    Lemon Potatoes,188
    Parmesan Baskets
    w/Savoury Tomato Egg
    Cups,55
    Pizzaola Hamburger
    Sliders,31
    Seafood Cioppino.156
    Seafood Lasagne,158
    Shrimp Caesar Pizza,161
    Tomato Confit,199
    Zucchini Towers,201

Bean Sprouts,
    Egg Foo Young Frittata,83

Bechamel Sauce,
    Lasagna Bolognese,94

Beef Broth,
    Bourguignon Sauce,204
    Butternut Squash
    Casserole,172
    French Onion Soup,22

Butternut Squash
Casserole,172
French Onion Soup,22
Macaroni & Cheese Beef
Hash with Eggs,53
Veal Chops in Marsala
Sauce,113

Beef Shanks,
Lasagna Bolognese,94

Beef Stock,
Cottage Pie,79
Goody Gouda Polenta183
Lasagna Bolognese,94
Pork Loins with Apple/
Cranberry Stuffing,99

Beer,
Cheddar Potato Soup,18
Chicken Prosciutto Pie,125
Savoury Mushroom
Strata,196

Beets,
Chilled Golden Beet &
Fennel Soup,20
Goat Cheese Cheescake
with Beets,181

Bison,
Bison Burgers,60

Black beans,
Huevos Rancheros,50
Mexican Cheese &
Chicken Dip,26
Spicy Black Bean Soup,37

Black olive,
Italian Pizza Custard,89
Polenta Crackers with
Sausage Meatballs,32

Black Truffles,
Foie Gras Brulee,21

Blackberries,
Foie Gras Brulee,21

Blue Cheese,
Bison Burgers,60
Blue Cheese
Coleslaw,168
Buffalo Chicken
Burgers,61

Blueberries,
Fruit Tart,226

Luscious Lemon Blueberry
Bread Pudding,231

Blue Corn Tortilla,
Chicken Meatballs
w/Pimento Cheese
Sauce,63
Mexican Cheese &
Chicken Dip,26
Pineapple Mango Duck
Nachos,30

Bourguignon,
Bourguignon Sauce,204
Lamb Bourguignon,93

Boursin,
Boursin Gallet,169

Brandied Butter
Mushrooms,170

Bread crumbs,
    Banana Cake,219
    Chicken Parmesan,123
    Halibut a la Parmesan,146
    Raspberry Coffee Cake,57
    Scallion Encrusted Rack
    of lamb,103

Breakfast,
    Breakfast Strata,42
    Eggs Two Ways,45

Brisket,77

Broccoli,
    Cheddar Broccoli & Rice
    Casserole,175
    Chicken Prosciutto Pie,125

Brown Rice,
    Cheddar Broccoli & Rice
    Casserole,175
    Chicken Prosciutto
    Pie,125
    De-constructed Stuffed
    Cabbage,81
    Fiesta Rice Egg Cups
    w/Jumbo Lump Crab,46
    Jambalaya,148
    Mexican Rice,190
    Poblanos stuffed with
    Chorizo
    and Shrimp,152
    Rice pudding,236

Brunch,
    Apricot Stuffed French
    Toast,41

Breakfast Strata,42
Carmel Apple Walnut
Topping for Pancakes,44
Eggs Two Ways,45
Fiesta Rice Egg Cups with
Jumbo Lump Crab,46
French Toast with Creme
Brulee Sauce,48
Huevos Rancheros,50
Italian Frittata,51
Macaroni & Cheese Beef
Hash with Eggs,53
Parmesan Baskets with
Savory Tomato Egg
Cups,55
Raspberry Coffee Cake,57

Brussels Sprouts,171

Burgers,
    Bison Burgers,60
    Buffalo Chicken
    Burgers,61
    Greek Style Lamb
    Burgers,67
    Pizzaola hamburger
    Sliders,29
    Sirloin Burgers,72

Butternut squash,
    Butternut squash
    casserole,172

Butterscotch Carmel topping,
    Godiva Carmel
    Cheesecake with
    Chocolate Cookies,227

C

Cabbage,
    Cabbage,169
    De-constructed Stuffed
    Cabbage,81

Cake
    Banana Cake,219
    Flourless Chocolate
    Kahlua Cake,224
    White Chocolate
Chambord
    Pudding Cake,238

Carrots,
    Bourguignon sauce,204
    Cottage Pie,79
    De-constructed Chicken
    Pot Pie,129
    Ginger Garlic Chicken
    Soup,24
    Lasagna Bolognese,94
    Stuffed meat Loaf,111

Champagne,
    Gruyere Scalloped
    Potatoes with Champagne
    Sauce,185

Cheesecake,
    Goat Cheese Cheescake
    with beets,181
    Godiva Carmel
    Cheesecake with
    Chocolate Cookies,227

Chicken,
    Black Forest Chicken,120
    Buffalo Chicken burgers,61
    Chicken Margarita,122

Chicken meatballs w/
Pimento
Cheese Sauce,63
Chicken on Horseback,64
Chicken Parmesan,123
Chicken Prosciutto Pie,125
Chinese Chicken Lettuce
Wraps,65
Creamy Chicken and
Mushroom Casserole,127
De-constructed Chicken
Pot Pie,129
Ginger Garlic Chicken
Soup,24
Inside out Cordon Blue
over Cheese Fettuccine,87
Italian Chicken Zucchini
Bundles,131
Lemon Chicken,133
Mexican Cheese &
Chicken Dip,26
Orange Garlic Five Spice
Injected Chicken,135
Tandoori Chicken with
Raita Sauce,137

Chocolate,
    Chocolate Cherry Semi-
    freddo,221
    Flourless Chocolate
    Kahlua Cake,224
    Godiva Carmel
    Cheesecake with
    Chocolate Cookies,227
    White Chocolate
    Chambord
    Pudding Cake,238

Cranberries,
    Orange Liqueur
    Cranberries,191
    Poached pears with
    Cranberries and Stilton
    Cheese,234
    Pork Loins with
    Apple/Cranberry
    Stuffing,99

D

Dessert,
    Apple Betty,217
    Banana Cake,219
    Chocolate Cherry Semi-
    freddo,221
    Creme Anglais,222
    Dulce de Leche,223
    Flourless Chocolate
    Kahlua cake,224
    Fruit Tart,226
    Godiva Carmel
    Cheesecake with
    Chocolate Cookies,227
    Gooey Cinnamon Brown
    Sugar Apples,229
    Key Lime Pie,230
    Luscious Lemon Blueberry
    Bread Pudding,231
    Peanut Butter and Apple
    Custard,232
    Poached Pears with
    Cranberries and
    Stilton Cheese,234
    Pumpkin Souffle,235
    Rice Pudding,236
    Vanilla Cherry
    Pudding,237
    White Chocolate Chambord
    Pudding Cake,238

Dinner,
    Asian Duck Breasts,118
    Chicken Margarita,122
    Chicken Parmesan,123
    Cottage Pie,79
    Eggplant Lasagna,85
    Flounder Stuffed with
    Crabmeat,143
    Garlic Ginger Fish
    w/Shitake
    Mushroom Soy Glaze,145
    Halibut a la Parmesan,146
    Pork Loins with
    Apple/Cranberry
    Stuffing,99
    Red Snapper Vera
    Cruz,155
    Reuben lasagna,101
    Scallion Encrusted Rack of
    lamb,103
    Stuffed center Cut Pork
    chops,109
    Tandoori Chicken with
    Raita
    Sauce,137
    Veal Chops in Marsala
    Sauce,113
    Veal Scallopine with
    Prosciutto and
    Asparagus,115
    Yummy Turkey Breast,139

Duck,
    Asian Duck Breasts,118
    Pineapple mango Duck
    Nachos,30

E

Eggs,
    Apricot Stuffed French
    Toast,41
    Breakfast Strata,42
    Egg Foo Young Frittata,83
    Eggs Two Ways,45
    Fiesta Rice Egg Cups with
    Jumbo Lump Crab,46
    French Toast with Creme
    Brulee Sauce,48
    Huevos Rancheros,50
    Italian Frittata,51
    Macaroni & Cheese Beef
    Hash
    with Eggs,53
    Parmesan Baskets
    w/Savory
    Tomato Egg Cups,55

Escargot,
    Garlic Escargot w/Kasseri
    Cheese,23

F

Fennel,
    Chilled Golden Beet &
    Fennel Soup,20
    Fennel & Onion
    Parmesan,179
    Greek Style Lamb
    Burgers,67

Feta Cheese,
    Red Snapper Vera
    Cruz,155

Fettuccine,
    Chicken Parmesan,123

Ginger Garlic Chicken
Soup,24
    Inside Out Cordon Blue
    over Cheese Fettuccine,87
    Lobster Newburg,150

Fingerling Potatoes,180

Fish,
    Flounder Stuffed with
    Crabmeat,143
    Garlic Ginger Fish
    w/Shitake Mushroom Soy
    Glaze,145
    Halibut a la Parmesan,146
    Red Grouper poached in
    Butter Sauce,154
    Red Snapper Vera
    Cruz,155
    Seafood Cioppino,156
    Tuna Casserole,164

Flour,
    De-constructed Chicken
    Pot Pie,129
    Puff Pastry,215

Flourless,
    Flourless Chocolate
    Kahlua Cake,224

French Onion Soup,22

French Toast,
    Apricot Stuffed French
    Toast,41
    French Toast with Creme
    Brulee Sauce,48

Fruit,
    Carmel Apple Walnut
    Topping for Pancakes,44
    Fruit Tart,226
    Orange Liqueur
    Cranberries,191

G

Garam masala,
    Tandoori Chicken with
    Raita Sauce,137

Garlic,
    Garlic Ginger Fish
    w/Shitake Mushroom
    Glaze,145
    Garlic Escargot w/ Kasseri
    Cheese,23
    Greek Style lamb
    Burgers,67
    Orange Garlic Five Spice
    Injected Chicken,135

Ginger,
    Chilled Golden Beet &
    Fennel Soup,20
    Chinese Chicken Lettuce
    Wraps,65
    Garlic Ginger Fish w/
    Shitake Mushroom Soy
    Glaze,145
    Pork & Shrimp
    Dumplings,34
    Spicy Chinese Short
    Ribs,107
    Tandoori Chicken with
    Raita sauce,137

Gluten Free,
    Flourless Chocolate
    Kahlua Cake,224
    Gluten Free Savoury
    Tomato &
    Onion Tart,213

Goat Cheese,
    Goat Cheese Cheesecake
    with Beets,181
    Stuffed Center Cut Pork
    Chops,109

Green Chile,
    Green Chile Mac &
    Cheese,184
    Poblanos stuffed with
    Chorizo and Shrimp,152
    Spicy green beans,198

Green Pepper,
    Sloppy Joes,73

Ground Beef,
    Coney sauce,206
    De-constructed Stuffed
    Cabbage,81
    Eggplant Lasagna,85
    Patti Melt,70
    Pizzaola Hamburger
    Sliders,31
    Sloppy Joes,73
    Stuffed Meat Loaf,111

Ground Pork,
    Pork & Shrimp
    Dumplings,34
    Stuffed Meat Loaf,111

Gruyere,
    Butternut Squash
    Casserole,172
    Cheddar Broccoli & Rice
    Casserole,175
    Creamy Chicken and Wild
    Mushroom Casserole,127
    French Onion Soup,22
    Gruyere Scalloped
    Potatoes with Champagne
    Sauce,185
    Inside out Cordon Bleu
    over Cheese Fettuccine,87

H

Halibut,
    Halibut a la Parmesan,146

Ham,
    Breakfast Strata,42
    Inside Out Cordon Bleu
    over Cheese fettuccine,87
    Pepper Jack Ham &
    Cauliflower Soup,29

Heavy Cream,
    Breakfast Strata,42
    Chocolate Cherry Semi-
    freddo,221
    Creme Anglais,222
    Espuma Wasabi
    Potatoes,177
    Foie Gras Brulee,21
    French Toast with Creme
    Brulee Sauce,48
    Lasagna Bolognese,94
    Luscious Lemon Blueberry
    Bread Pudding,231
    Pepper Jack Ham &
    Cauliflower Soup,29

Savoury Mushroom
    Strata,196
    Vanilla Cherry
    Pudding,237
    Vichyssoise,39

Hoisin Sauce,
    Asian Duck breasts,118
    Spicy Chinese Short
    Ribs,107

Horseradish,
    Blue Cheese Coleslaw,168
    Cottage Pie,79

Hot dogs,
    Coney Dog Casserole,78
    Coney Sauce,206

Hot Italian Sausage,
    Italian Frittata,51

Hot Sauce,
    Buffalo Chicken
    Burgers,61
    Halibut a la Parmesan,146
    Mexican Cheese &
    Chicken Dip,26
    Spinach Artichoke Dip,38

Huevos Rancheros,50

I

Injected,
    Orange Garlic Five Spice
    Injected Chicken,135

Italian,
    Italian Chicken Zucchini
    Bundles,131

Italian Frittata,51
Italian Pizza Custard,89
Italian Portabellos,91

Italian Sausage,
  Eggplant Lasagna,85
  Italian Frittata,51
  Italian Portabellos,91
  Polenta Crackers with
  Sausage & Meatballs,32
  Spaghetti Casserole,105

J

Jambalaya,148

K

Kasseri Cheese,
  Garlic Escargot w/Kasseri
  Cheese,23

Ketchup,
  Coney Dog Casserole,78
  Pork & Shrimp
  Dumplings,34
  Sloppy Joes,73
  Spicy Chinese Short
  Ribs,107

Key Lime,
  Key Lime Pie,230

Kicked up Corn on the
Cob,187

Kielbasa sausage,
  Black Forest Chicken
  Stew,120

Kiwi,
  Fruit Tart,226

L

Lamb,
  Cottage Pie,79
  Greek Style Lamb
  Burgers,67
  Gyros with Tzatziki
  Sauce,68
  Lamb Bourguignon,93
  Scallion Encrusted Rack of
  Lamb,103

Leeks,
  Cheddar potato Soup,18
  Egg Foo Young,83
  Ginger Garlic Chicken
  Soup,24
  Gruyere Scalloped
  Potatoes with Champagne
  Sauce,185
  Pepper Jack Ham &
  Cauliflower Soup,29
  Vegetable Medeley
  Casserole,200
  Vichyssoise,39

Lemon,
  Lemon Chicken,133
  Lemon Potatoes,188
  Lemon Tarragon Potato
  Salad,189
  Luscious Lemon Blueberry
  Bread Pudding,231
  Mussels in Lemon Grass
  Curry Coconut Broth,27
  Red Grouper poached in
  Butter sauce,154

Lemon Basil,
    Seafood Cioppino,156
    Seafood Lasagne,158
    Shrimp Caesar Pizza,161

Lettuce leaves,
    Chinese Chicken Lettuce
    Wraps,65

Lobster,
    Lobster,149
    Lobster Newburg,150
    Seafood Lasagne,158

Low fat cream cheese,
    Apricot Stuffed French
    Toast,41
    Black Forest Chicken
    Stew,120
    Boursin Gallet,169
    Buffalo Chicken
    Burgers,61
    Cheddar Broccoli & Rice
    Casserole,175
    Cheddar Potato Soup,18
    Chicken Prosciutto
    Pie,125
    Creamy Chicken and Wild
    Mushroom
    Casserole,127
    Flounder stuffed with
    Crabmeat,143
    Goat Cheese Cheesecake
    with Beets,181
    Godiva Carmel
    Cheesecake with
    Chocolate Cookies,227
    Gooey Cinnamon Brown
    Sugar Apples,229
    Green Chile Mac &
    Cheese,184

Inside Out Cordon Blue
with
    Cheese Fettuccine,87
    Italian Chicken Zucchini
    Bundles,131
    Italian Pizza Custard,89
    Lasagna Bolognese,94
    Lemon Chicken,133
    Lobster Newburg,150
    Macaroni & Cheese Beef
    Hash with Eggs,53
    Parmesan Sauce,207
    Peanut Butter & Apple
    Custard,232
    Pepper Jack Ham &
    Cauliflower Soup,29
    Pimento Cheese
    Sauce,208
    Reuben Lasagna,101
    Rutabaga Souffle,194
    Spinach Artichoke Dip,38
    Stuffed Center Cut Pork
    Chops,109
    Tuna Casserole,164

Lump Crabmeat,
    Fiesta Rice Egg Cups
    w/Jumbo Lump Crab,46
    Flounder Stuffed with
    Crabmeat,143
    Seafood Lasagne,158

M

Macaroni,
    Green Chile Mac &
    Cheese,184
    Macaroni & Cheese Beef
    Hash with Eggs,53

Maderia,
    Pheasant with Orange
    Maderia
    Sauce,136

Marinara Sauce,
    Italian Frittata,51
    Spaghetti Casserole,105

Mashed Potatoes,
    Cottage Pie,79

Mayonnaise,
    Halibut a la Parmesan,146
    Lemon Tarragon Potato
    Salad,189
    Pimento Cheese
    sauce,208
    Scallion Encrusted Rack
    of Lamb,103
    Spinach Artichoke Dip,38

Meatballs,
    Chicken Meatballs
    w/Pimento Cheese
    Sauce,63
    Polenta Crackers with
    Sausage & Meatballs,32

Mexican Rice,
    Mexican Rice,190
    South of the Border
    Shrimp and Sausage
    Soup,36

Monterey Jack,
    Poblanos stuffed with
    Chorizo and Shrimp,152

Mozzarella,
    Pizzaola Hamburger
    Sliders,31

Mushrooms,
    Brandied Butter
    Mushrooms,170
    Chinese Chicken Lettuce
    Wraps,65
    Creamy Chicken and Wild
    Mushroom Casserole, 127
    Italian Portabellos,91
    Savoury Mushroom
    Strata,196
    Tuna Casserole,164

Mussels,
    Mussels in Lemon Curry
    Coconut Broth,27
    Seafood Cioppino,156
    Spanish Paella,162

N

Noodles,
    Chinese Chicken Lettuce
    Wraps,65
    Creamy Chicken and Wild
    Mushroom Casserole,127
    Lamb Bourguignon,93
    Lasagna Bolognese,94
    Seafood Lasagne,158
    Tuna casserole,164

O

Old Bay Seasoning,
    Red Bliss Potatoes
    w/onions,193

Olive Oil,
Tomato Confit,199

Onion,
Fennel & Onion a la
Parmesan,179
French Onion Soup,22

Onion Soup Mix,
Brisket,77
Stuffed Meat Loaf,111
Yummy Turkey Breast,139

Orange,
Chilled Golden Beet &
Fennel Soup,20
Orange Garlic Five Spice
Injected Chicken,135
Orange Liqueur
Cranberries,191
Pheasant with Orange
Maderia Sauce,136
Pork Loins with Apple/
Cranberry Stuffing,99

P

Pappardelle noodles,
Lamb Bourguignon,93

Parmesan,
Chicken Parmesan,123
Fennel & Onion
Parmesan,179
Gruyere Scalloped
Potatoes with
Champagne Sauce,185
Halibut a la Parmesan,146
Parmesan Baskets
w/Savoury
Tomato Egg Cups,55

Parmesan Sauce,207
Parmesan Truffle
Fries,192

Peanut butter,
Peanut Butter & Apple
Custard,232

Pears,
Poached Pears with
Cranberries and Stilton
cheese,234

Peas,
Cottage Pie,79
Ginger Garlic Chicken
Soup,24
Lobster Newburg,150

Pepper Jack Cheese,
Pepper Jack Ham &
Cauliflower Soup,29
Sloppy Joes,73
Stuffed Meat Loaf,111

Pepperoni,
Italian Chicken Zucchini
Bundles,131
Italian Frittata,51
Italian Pizza Custard,89
Italian Portabellos,91
Pizzaola Hamburger
Sliders,31
Zucchini Towers,201

Peppers,
Bison Burgers,60
Fiesta Rice Egg Cups
w/Jumbo
Lump Crab,46

Flounder Stuffed with
Crabmeat,143
Lobster Newburg,150
Red Snapper Vera
Cruz,155
Seafood Cioppino,156
Shrimp Caesar Pizza,161
Sloppy Joes,73
Spanish Paella,162
Stuffed Meat Loaf,111
Tandoori Chicken with
Raita
Sauce,137

Pesto,
Chicken Margarita,122
Mussels in Lemon Grass
Curry
Coconut Broth,27
Parmesan Baskets
w/Savoury
Tomato Egg Cups,55
Polenta Crackers with
Sausage & Meatballs,32

Pie crust,
Gluten Free Savoury
Tomato &
Onion Tart,213

Pimento,
Chicken Meatballs
w/Pimento Cheese
Sauce,63
Pimento Cheese
Sauce,208

Pineapple,
Boursin Gallet,169
Pineapple Mango Duck
Nachos,30

Pinto beans,
Mexican Rice,190
Pineapple mango Duck
Nachos,30

Pistachio nuts,
Goat Cheese Cheesecake
with
Beets,181

Pork,
Egg Foo Young Frittata,83
Lasagna Bolognese,94
Pork & Shrimp
Dumplings,34
Pork Loins with
Apple/Cranberry
Stuffing,99
Sante Fe Pork Tacos,71
Stuffed Center Cut Pork
Chops,109
Stuffed Meat Loaf,111

Potato,
Boursin Gallet,169
Cheddar Potato Soup,18
Cottage Pie,79
Espuma Wasabi
Potatoes,177
Fingerling Potatoes,180
Gruyere Scalloped
Potatoes with Champagne
Sauce,185
Lemon Potatoes,188
Lemon Tarragon Potato
Salad,189
Parmesan Truffle
Fries,192
Red Bliss Potatoes
w/onions,193
Reuben Lasagna,101

Vichyssoise,39

Prosciutto,
    Chicken Margarita,122
    Chicken Prosciutto
    Pie,125
    Veal Scallopine with
    Prosciutto
    and Asparagus,115

Provolone,
    Chicken Margarita,122
    Patti Melt,70

Puff Pastry,
    De-constructed Chicken
    Pot Pie,129
    Puff Pastry,215

Q

Quinoa,
    Butternut Squash
    Casserole,172

R

Raisins,
    Rice Pudding,236

Raita Sauce,
    Tandoori Chicken with
Raita
    Sauce,137
Ranch Dressing,
    Buffalo Chicken
Burgers,61

Raspberries,
    Flourless Chocolate
    Kahlua Cake,224

White Chocolate
Chamboard Pudding
Cake,238

Red Wine,
    Bourguignon Sauce,204
    Lasagna Bolognese,94
    Poached Pears with
    Cranberries and Stilton
    Cheese,234
    Red Wine Sauce,209

Rice,
    Cheddar Broccoli & Rice
    Casserole,175
    Fiesta Rice Egg Cups
    w/Jumbo Lump Crab,46
    Mexican Rice,190
    Rice Pudding,236

Ricotta,
    Eggplant Lasagna,85
    Italian Pizza Custard,89
    Italian Portabellos,91
    Lasagna Bolognese,94

S

Sage,
    Dressing/Stuffing,176

Salad,
    Blue Cheese
    Coleslaw,168
    Salsa,
    Huevos Rancheros,50
    Pineapple Mango Duck
    Nachos,30
    Sante Fe Pork Tacos,71
    Spicy Black Bean Soup,37

Sauerkraut,
    Black Forest Chicken
    Stew,120
    Reuben Lasagna,101

Shrimp,
    Jambalaya,148
    Poblanos stuffed with
    Chorizo and Shrimp,152
    Pork & Shrimp
    Dumplings,34
    Seafood Cioppino,156
    Seafood Lasagna,158
    Shrimp & Sausage,160
    Shrimp Caesar Pizza,161
    South of the Border
    Shrimp and Sausage
    Soup,36
    Spanish Paella,162

Slivered almonds,
    Vanilla Cherry
    Pudding,237

Soup,
    Cheddar Potato Soup,18
    Chilled Golden Beet &
    Fennel Soup,20
    Ginger Garlic Chicken
    Soup,24
    Pepper Jack Ham &
    Cauliflower Soup,29
    South of the Border
    Shrimp and Sausage
    Soup,36
    Spicy Black bean Soup,37
    Vichyssoise,39

Sour cream,
    Chilled Golden Beet &
    fennel Soup,20

Goat Cheese Cheesecake
    with Beets,181
    Mexican Cheese &
    Chicken Dip,26
    Sante Fe Pork Tacos,71

Soy Sauce,
    Chinese Chicken Lettuce
    Wraps,65
    Garlic Ginger Fish
    w/Shitake
    Mushroom Soy Glaze,145
    Pork Loins with Apple/
    Cranberry Stuffing,99

Spinach,
    Parmesan Baskets
    w/Savoury
    Tomato Egg Cups,55
    Spaghetti Casserole,105
    Spinach Artichoke Dip,38
    Stuffed Center Cut Pork
    Chops,109
    Vegetable Medeley
    Casserole,200

Stove Top,
    Bourguignon Sauce,204
    Coney sauce,206
    Cornstarch Crepes,211
    Mexican Rice,190
    Red Wine Sauce,209

Strawberries,
    Fruit Tart,226

Sun-dried Tomatoes,
    Breakfast Strata,42
    Chicken Meatballs
    w/Pimento
    Cheese Sauce,63

Chicken on Horseback,64
Pizzaola Hamburger
Sliders,31
Polenta Crackers with
Sausage
& Meatballs,32
Stuffed Center Cut Pork
Chops,109

T

Taco seasoning,
Sante Fe Pork Tacos,71

Thousand Island Dressing,
Reuben Lasagna,101

Tomato Sauce,
Chicken Parmesan,123
Coney Sauce,206
Lasagna Bolognese,94
Seafood Cioppino,156

Tomato soup,
De-constructed Stuffed
Cabbage,81
Mexican Rice,190

Tortillas,
Chicken Meatballs
w/Pimento Cheese
Sauce,63
Huevos Rancheros,50

Turkey Gravy,
Egg Foo Young,83

V

Vanilla,
Vanilla Cherry
Pudding,237

Veal,
Veal Chops in Marsala
Sauce,113
Veal Scallopine with
Prosciutto
and Asparagus.115

W

Walnuts,
Banana Cake,219
Carmel Apple Walnut
Topping for Pancakes,44
French Toast with Creme
Brulee Sauce,48
Poached Pears with
Cranberries and Stilton
Cheese,234
Raspberry Coffee Cake,57

Water Chestnuts,
Chinese Chicken Lettuce
Wraps,65
Egg Foo Young Frittata,83
Pork & Shrimp
Dumplings,34

Worcestershire Sauce,
De-constructed Stuffed
Cabbage,81
Flounder Stuffed with
Crabmeat,143
French Onion Soup,22
Pork & Shrimp
Dumplings,34

Savoury Mushroom
Strata,196
Sirloin Burgers,72

Y

Yukon Gold Potatoes,
Gruyere Scalloped
Potatoes with Champagne
Sauce,185
Lemon Potatoes,188
Lemon Tarragon Potato
Salad,189

Z

Zucchini,
Italian Chicken Zucchini
Bundles,131
Zucchini Towers,201

5761761R00143

Printed in Great Britain
by Amazon.co.uk, Ltd.,
Marston Gate.